CCCC STUDIES IN WRITING & RH

*Edited by Steve Parks, University of *

The aim of the CCCC Studies in Writing & Rhetoric (SWR) Series is to influence how we think about language in action and especially how writing gets taught at the college level. The methods of studies vary from the critical to historical to linguistic to ethnographic, and their authors draw on work in various fields that inform composition—including rhetoric, communication, education, discourse analysis, psychology, cultural studies, and literature. Their focuses are similarly diverse—ranging from individual writers and teachers, to work on classrooms and communities and curricula, to analyses of the social, political, and material contexts of writing and its teaching.

SWR was one of the first scholarly book series to focus on the teaching of writing. It was established in 1980 by the Conference on College Composition and Communication (CCCC) in order to promote research in the emerging field of writing studies. As our field has grown, the research sponsored by SWR has continued to articulate the commitment of CCCC to supporting the work of writing teachers as reflective practitioners and intellectuals.

We are eager to identify influential work in writing and rhetoric as it emerges. We thus ask authors to send us project proposals that clearly situate their work in the field and show how they aim to redirect our ongoing conversations about writing and its teaching. Proposals should include an overview of the project, a brief annotated table of contents, and a sample chapter. They should not exceed 10,000 words.

To submit a proposal, please register as an author at www.editorial manager.com/nctebp. Once registered, follow the steps to submit a proposal (be sure to choose SWR Book Proposal from the drop-down list of article submission types).

WRITING PROGRAMS, VETERANS STUDIES, AND THE POST-9/11 UNIVERSITY

A FIELD GUIDE

D. Alexis Hart
Allegheny College

Roger Thompson
Stony Brook University

Conference on College
Composition and
Communication

National Council of
Teachers of English

Staff Editor: Bonny Graham
Series Editor: Steve Parks
Interior Design: Mary Rohrer
Cover Design: Pat Mayer
Cover Photo: Shannon P. Meehan

NCTE Stock Number: 75057; eStock Number: 75064
ISBN 978-0-8141-7505-7; eISBN 978-0-8141-7506-4

It is the policy of NCTE in its journals and other publications to provide a forum for the open discussion of ideas concerning the content and the teaching of English and the language arts. Publicity accorded to any particular point of view does not imply endorsement by the Executive Committee, the Board of Directors, or the membership at large, except in announcements of policy, where such endorsement is clearly specified.

NCTE provides equal employment opportunity (EEO) to all staff members and applicants for employment without regard to race, color, religion, sex, national origin, age, physical, mental or perceived handicap/disability, sexual orientation including gender identity or expression, ancestry, genetic information, marital status, military status, unfavorable discharge from military service, pregnancy, citizenship status, personal appearance, matriculation or political affiliation, or any other protected status under applicable federal, state, and local laws.

Every effort has been made to provide current URLs and email addresses, but because of the rapidly changing nature of the web, some sites and addresses may no longer be accessible.

Library of Congress Cataloging-in-Publication Data

A catalog record for this book has been requested.

For
Captain Daddy Bud Hart, Alexis's military and professorial role model; Captain Shannon Meehan, who launched Roger on this journey; and all student veterans and those who aid their success, as writers and beyond

CONTENTS

"AMERICAN CULTURE IS, at this time, a culture of war."

So write Alexis Hart and Roger Thompson in this insightful and thoroughly practicable guide to teasing stories out of American student veterans. They are quite right, it is a culture of war, though one typical of our times, another facet of our consumption.

Twenty-first-century American war culture is a war to binge watch on YouTube. It's a war in Marvel Universes, where the bad guys are both bad and helpfully uniformed. It's a *Call of Duty* war, and a Thank You for Your Service before football games war, and a camo leggings at Forever 21 war, and a Facebook post to remember that #21VeteransADay commit suicide war.

This war is certainly—and fortunately, this must be said up front—not an experience to be lived war, at least not by the vast majority of Americans.

And therein yawns the gap.

In modern parlance, we often call this the civilian-military divide—though as any refugee escaping conflict can tell you, it is really a division between anyone who has felt the terror of personal violence and those who haven't. This gap has felt particularly acute over the last twenty years; America does not tell a shared wartime story. "After 9/11, the military went to war, but America went to the mall," goes the old refrain.

The phenomenon isn't new; as long as humans have fought war in a place other than their homes, there has existed an experiential division between those who fight the war and those who send them. What is new is not the gap, then, but the contemporary illusion that the gap can be bridged by sufficient quantities of consumer electronics. That the internet can bring us together in moments of shared empathy, and that therefore, by extension, if I play enough levels of the latest *Modern Warfare* I know what the real thing feels like. The mirror and the image get confused.

This illusion is only challenged in those few places where civilians and veterans mingle and share ideas. Which is why if we truly want to work on closing this divide in our country, college classrooms will be one of the best places to do it.

Over the last several decades, universities have begun to seek diversity as an inherent good, and veterans going back to school have been swept up in this effort, for reasons altruistic and financially cynical, as the Post-9/11 GI Bill has both greatly expanded educational opportunities for veterans and offered a tuition windfall to higher education institutions.

Including veteran status as marking diversity—in the same way as do race, gender, and sexual orientation, for example—has always made me personally uncomfortable. After all, unlike other demographic groups (many, but not all, of which are also federally protected classes), being a veteran is self-chosen,[1] at least as long as we have an all-volunteer military.

But I can see the argument. Veterans do genuinely add to the diversity of a campus and help break down, at least slightly, the civilian-military divide. It is easier to separate than unite, though, so that civ-mil chasm is shrunk only fitfully, one by one, as veterans sit next to traditional college students and maybe even have conversations.

No matter what their branch of service or specific story, nearly all veterans have had experiences in their past that distinguish them from average 18-year-olds. Veterans are almost always at least four years older, and in that added time have moved from their hometowns to new parts of the United States, have perhaps lived in foreign countries, learned to be in a minority ignorant of the local languages, become aware of the economic abundance of the United States. College is not their first time away from home.

None of this is to imply that veterans themselves reach college with a united or "typical" experience. As Hart and Thompson note, the term *veteran* itself is hardly precise, considering a wide range of possible backgrounds. Not only does each service—Army, Navy, Air Force, Marine Corps, Coast Guard—have its own distinct culture, geography, and, in a real sense, language, but the dispersed nature of our technological society and the geographic spread of the "War on Terror" have put to bed any notion of a cohesive veteran experience. A drone pilot in Nevada sees more "combat" than a gate guard stuck on a large logistics base in central Iraq.

So, what, if anything, does unite today's veterans?

In his survey of Iraq and Afghanistan war literature for the *New Yorker,* George Packer argues that the uniting image or symbol of this war—like the trench for World War I and the jungle for Vietnam—is the homecoming. No matter where we went, and no matter what we did, we all came home, vertical or horizontal. And more than that, because the wars in Afghanistan and Iraq and Pakistan and Syria and Libya and Somalia continue, we all came home alone. We all chose when to end our wars. Or we chose to do our time and exit the service before facing the crucible of the combat zone at all. How and where and why we made that decision, how we decided to come home, well, that's the topic of much of today's modern war literature.

The second uniting factor is the real sense, and perhaps in many cases a factually accurate one, that whatever we did before we came home—going on patrol in Kunar province or fixing a nuclear weapon in Nevada or saving someone's life in a canal in Tal Afar or building an Ebola clinic in Liberia—we have already peaked out. That the most important things we will ever do in our lives we have already done by the age of twenty-five.

Oh, what a burden this is.

Sometimes I am invited to speak at colleges, to "explain" veterans to the well-meaning-but-a-little-lost administrators. And at first, I wondered what I should say. How can veterans be so different? After all, we are not space aliens with twelve heads.

But here we have landed at the key point. For university professors: How to make Psych 101 feel as relevant and important as the last six years of that veteran's life. How to show her that even better opportunities are possible on the other side. How to teach him to buckle down and not give up. How to show that writing their story is key to this journey.

How to do that? Some of those answers are in this book.

Brian Castner
October 1, 2019
Grand Island, New York

ACKNOWLEDGMENTS

WE SIMPLY DO NOT HAVE ROOM to acknowledge everyone who has helped us in this project. We have benefited from the generosity of time, resources, energy, and spirit of so many people and organizations that virtually every day we are humbled by the opportunity to do this work. We gratefully acknowledge the generative support of the CCCC Research Grant—the funding that launched us. We thank colleagues and mentors at the Inaugural Dartmouth Summer Seminar for Composition Research (2011), which challenged us to push this project beyond our initial vision. We thank Steve Parks, who enthusiastically ushered us through revisions and who challenged our thinking more than once, and we acknowledge the very productive guidance from the peer reviewers of this manuscript. Thanks to Bonny Graham and the rest of the SWR team for their hard work in bringing this volume to print on a ridiculous timeline. Our deepest gratitude goes to all the people we met on our site visits and the interviewees who gave us their time and shared their stories with us—you were gracious and helpful without fail, and often you greeted us despite no forewarning. Thank you. We thank the members of the Writing with Current, Former, and Future Members of the Military Standing Group who have encouraged us along the way, and the members of the Veterans in Society professional Facebook group. To all the academic support committees that do important work day in and day out without much notice—we see you, and we know we aren't successful without your contributions. To our supportive colleagues at VMI, thanks for your help in the early stages of this project. It meant a lot to us in a time of trials. To that one special Team at VMI—we adore you. Thanks for pushing us along. To our colleagues and students at Allegheny and Stony Brook, thank you for your support.

Alexis: Special thanks to Mike, Amelia, and Agatha for giving me time and space to work on this project and the love and support I needed to carry on. And thanks to Roger, my dedicated collaborator in research and writing; I couldn't have done it without you, pardn'r.

Roger: I can't say thank you enough to Alan Baragona—your mentorship and encouragement pushed this along. The book doesn't exist without you. To all those cadets and student veterans who helped us with this project, thank you. You've made me not only a better teacher and scholar, but also a better person. For my family, especially Kim (who is my greatest writerly advocate) and Ethan, I can't say I love you enough. To the Meehan clan—this one's for you. And, finally, thanks to Alexis—I can only say that this journey has proven what an exceptional talent and colleague you are. You can stop pretending you're not.

INTRODUCTION: THEORIZING THE POST-9/11 VETERAN

WRITING FOR A VETERANS DAY SPEECH at Stony Brook University, Sherry Shi, a veteran and SBU graduate, describes how the extensive training she received for her Military Occupational Specialty (MOS), intelligence analyst, prepared her for deployment to Iraq. She notes, however, "In Iraq, I was actually assigned to many duties that did not pertain to my occupation specialty." Shi's statement certainly reflects typical military service, especially during a deployment, but it is also a striking parallel to the way student veterans often feel when, after a career in the military, they encounter new roles as students and civilians. In that transition, they inevitably face new duties that do not pertain to their MOS and even seem well outside their military training more broadly.

The transition from the military to civilian life has been widely represented in popular culture over time, with writers like Bryan Doerries locating such representations as far back as ancient Greece. Doerries has translated and staged dramatic readings of ancient Greek plays in a wide variety of communities in the United States and abroad in order to prompt discussion about the difficulty of veterans' transitions and, indeed, the challenges of being a "veteran" altogether. His work, and many others', has helped local communities explore the dissonance veterans feel when moving from their roles as service members to their roles as family members, community members, and employees outside of the military. More important, it has helped communities explore the nature of "the veteran" itself.

Within the academy, a growing body of scholarship from a wide range of disciplines has theorized the nature of "the veteran" in American culture. This burgeoning scholarly interest in veterans is undoubtedly a legacy of the two wars the United States waged beginning in 2001. Operation Enduring Freedom (OEF) in Afghanistan and Operation Iraqi Freedom (OIF) engaged Americans in more than a decade of combat, among them a generation of people who either served in the military during war or witnessed these wars in unprecedented ways through evolving media technologies that made distant combat more visible than ever before. Notwithstanding the nominal ends of these wars, conflicts overseas involving US service personnel persist, and the aftermath of extended military engagement continues to resonate throughout our society. Indeed, our entire country has felt the impact of war. Nightly news broadcasts continue to highlight veterans and service members in human interest segments, the publishing industry continues to market books about war—both nonfiction and fiction, highlighting recent wars and historical ones—and American fascination with movies depicting international conflict, terrorism, and intense combat has perhaps never been higher. The media spotlight on the wars has been virtually impossible to escape, and the result is that American culture is, at this time, a culture of war.

This study is one of many attempts to understand that culture of war but is the first to provide an introduction to a nascent field of scholarly inquiry, veterans studies, and how it has been developed with remarkable force within the writing studies community. We do not claim to provide an exhaustive survey of all of the varied types of research that investigate military culture, the nature of war, or the ideology of international conflict. Nor do we claim to provide a definitive survey of scholarship on veterans. Instead, we aim to offer a critical account of the particular ways in which veterans studies has emerged within the discipline of writing studies. That accounting will detail why writing studies in particular seems to host so much of the research around veterans' issues in higher education and why scholars trained in fields like rhetoric or composition continue to push the development of this new field. In doing so, we also hope to demonstrate that maintaining a relationship with the field of veterans studies offers unique opportunities both to work across scholarly disciplines and to engage with broader academic and nonacademic communities. We believe studying the idea of "the veteran" mandates connection to and discussion with communities of veterans, and it is that feature of veterans studies that has, we will argue, so deeply engaged writing scholars.

Any attempt to define an interdisciplinary field will ultimately fail to capture the range of activities and motivations animating it, but rhetoric, a discipline that first rose to prominence in ancient Greece and other regions around the globe, continues to provide core aspects of education throughout most universities. Because it rests at the intersections of reading, writing, listening, speaking, and critical thinking, the study of rhetoric provides fertile territory for cross-disciplinary instruction and research. Indeed, writing studies as a prominent home for the study of rhetoric in universities has been so variously defined (Swearingen; Kopelson; Phelps and Ackerman; Mueller; Malenczyk et al.) that it makes some sense that interdisciplinary work finds a ready home among its practitioners. While we recognize the complex histories surrounding homes for rhetoric, composition, and writing within North American universities, for the purposes of our study we use "writing studies" (WS) to refer to the field that encapsulates them. We see this as the best way to include the wide range of theoretical configurations and departmental realities for writing teachers and researchers, even as we recognize its tentative adoption among some scholars and practitioners.

If WS as an interdisciplinary conceptualization of a field complicates its parameters and definitions, veterans studies' place within it is no different. For example, veterans may take first-year writing at different types of institutions—from community colleges to four-year baccalaureate colleges, to regional comprehensive universities, to research-intensive PhD-granting institutions, to online for-profit and not-for-profit institutions (McMurray; United States Congress, *For Profit*; Patton; Raab; Wong; L. Nelson; Salemme; Jones and Garrity). They may also take these courses at a military facility (or even on board a ship!) while on active duty (K. Wilson et al.; McGregor and Fernandez). Alternatively, they may receive credit for "College Composition" by passing a College Level Examination Program (CLEP) exam[1] or another equivalency exam. The types of faculty teaching first-year writing courses vary considerably, as well, ranging from no faculty (exam-based or independent study), to contingent faculty, to graduate student teaching assistants, to full-time lecturers and instructors, to tenure-track and tenured faculty. To complicate matters further, those teaching the courses may have little to no background or training in writing pedagogy (Karaali). Clearly, the variables are both complex and complicated, and make defining a field of study both impossible and undesirable—impossible because of the range of experiences; undesirable because of the potential harm done by generalizing a definition and applying it to distinct and distinctive situations.

Even so, scholarship in WS has in many respects led the way in providing core concepts for more nuanced engagement with veterans on college campuses. For example, the field has identified concepts like "residence time" that offer a framework to rethink veteran transition to civilian life as something other than a singular moment (Doe and Doe), drawn attention to writing classrooms as the location of the emergence of war trauma (Valentino, "Serving"; Lucas), and pointed to the way that student veterans mirror adult learner populations in first-year writing classrooms (Navarre Cleary). Scholars and teachers in WS have led the creation of veterans studies degree plans, launched a scholarly journal dedicated to veterans studies, and developed community writing initiatives that have become models of service learning and community engagement emulated around the country. If writing studies is not the heart of veteran studies as a field, it is its lifeblood, nourishing an interdisciplinary movement by focusing on student achievement and well-being through the discipline of writing.

This is probably not surprising given that WS scholars and faculty tend to have a commitment to first-year writing and general education requirements, and most student veterans must complete coursework in writing. Few other fields have comparable requirements shared among all undergraduates, regardless of degree or major. Because most undergraduate students are at some point required to take introductory and/or upper-division writing-intensive classes—most of which have comparatively small enrollments—writing faculty often find themselves becoming a point of first contact (indeed in some instances filling the role of "first responder" [De La Ysla]) for veterans at institutions of higher learning. That contact has shaped (and might even be described as the initial reason for) the rise of veterans studies among WS faculty. The same is likely less true for other faculty, whose specializations may limit the frequency or intensity of faculty–student veteran interaction. Further, while some other general education faculty, such as those in math, might have greater chances of interacting with student veterans, the nature of the coursework may lead to fewer disclosures of veteran status. By contrast—and as we'll examine throughout this volume—writing classrooms are by their nature the location of disclosures, regardless of the types of assignments faculty may use.

The surge of scholarly interest in veterans, of course, runs concurrent with the return of military personnel to the civilian world, and the desire to connect with veteran communities is at the heart of much of the recent scholarship. By the ten-year anniversary of September 11, 2001, more than 1.3 million service personnel had left the military (National Economic Council). Such a migration back to civilian life is bound to draw the attention of many of us, and higher education in particular has had to account for a dramatic demographic shift at our institutions and within our communities. The burgeoning scholarly interest in veterans, then, mirrors the increasing number of veterans who have matriculated into US colleges and universities. In 2013, the Veterans Administration reported that nearly 1.1 million beneficiaries were using some form of VA education benefits, with Post-9/11 GI Bill beneficiaries accounting for 750,000 of them ("Education" 8, 10). These numbers have climbed steadily since the end of official combat operations in Iraq and Afghanistan. While these numbers include officers who have used their benefits to attain graduate degrees (either face-to-face or online)[2] and dependents (spouses and children) to whom the benefits have been transferred, many former enlisted personnel have enrolled at community colleges, sought online degrees, or pursued their bachelor's degrees at traditional brick-and-mortar institutions, and during that process, teachers and researchers have increasingly come to know them and their stories. Not surprisingly, because of the relatively small enrollments and the prevalence of student-faculty conferences in writing courses, writing studies professionals have had particularly rich opportunities to make these connections and hear these narratives. Without that contact, it is virtually impossible to imagine the birth of veterans studies.

Nevertheless, the field is not yet fully defined, and part of our purpose in this volume is to build an initial architecture of the field based on specific scholarly and community developments in writing programs across the country. Accordingly, we examine not only academic inquiry into the idea of "the veteran," but also the concrete ways that veteran culture has been fostered or challenged in writing classrooms, in writing centers, and in college communities more generally. To illustrate those concrete methods, we provide examples of writing practices within the classroom and within the military, and we offer guidance for how best to implement strategies that emphasize veteran assets in the classroom. We thus imagine this text as a kind of field guide that, on the one hand, provides conceptual frameworks, but, on the other hand, provides concrete examples and guidance for faculty and researchers that they can adapt and apply to their local contexts. Further, we also describe some of the physical spaces that have been created for veterans, and we inquire into the conceptual frameworks that drive the creation of those spaces. Such spaces signal a noteworthy fascination with and catering to veterans and illustrate the complex ways that the idea of "the veteran" has manifested itself on college campuses. To understand those spaces is to understand how universities have attempted to integrate or assimilate veterans into campus cultures. Perhaps more important, these efforts illustrate the degree to which veterans have been marked as a distinctive student population. Whether or not they should be is at the heart of this study.

"THE VETERAN," COMBAT, AND THE EVASIVENESS OF DEFINITIONS

Any attempt to study veterans comes immediately upon a significant problem: what is "a veteran"? To whom can we apply the term and what are the characteristics of a person bearing this label?

One might imagine that a definition as simple as "a veteran is a person who has previously served in the military" would function as an effective synopsis, but it remains decidedly insufficient as a working definition. Former service members who receive other-than-honorable discharges, for example, are not eligible for veterans' benefits, including the GI Bill.[3] In addition, recent debates about agency around the term *veteran* attest to the stakes involved when veteran status is ascribed to or claimed by individuals. For example, the findings of the 2012 report "California's Women Veterans" shows that women who have served in the military often do not self-identify as "veterans" (Blanton and Foster 15). Similarly, college students with prior military service may or may not choose to self-identify as "veterans" and may not be using military benefits to finance their education, further complicating administrative efforts to identify them. Therefore, when colleges and universities attempt to provide services for veterans, or when academics attempt to study the military experience, a general definition is effectively useless, not because it is inaccurate, but because it cannot contain the diversity of experiences being referred to when discussions of veterans take place in communities, on college campuses, in classrooms, in policy boardrooms, or within the military itself. "The veteran," in other words, is anything but a stable term.

Even beyond the question of whether a person self-identifies as a veteran or whether a government body or a university might label someone a veteran, distinctions within the military complicate easy assignation of the term. Different veterans' experiences complicate simple definitions, whether prescriptive or descriptive. For instance, the experience of a combat Marine who served during the battle of Fallujah in 2004 is significantly different from that of the Army quartermaster who served at Ft. Hood at precisely the same time.[4] Similarly, the person who served in peacetime during the 1980s is unlikely to be regarded (or to regard themself) as "a veteran" in the same sense as someone who served during Operation Desert Storm in the 1990s. Significant distinctions between the different branches of service destabilize the term even more: does one include the Coast Guard in consideration of veterans? Or the

National Guard? What does it mean to be a seaman or an airman? What distinguishes a Marine from a soldier and why does it matter? Further, the notorious gap between officers and enlisted personnel, reified within military hierarchies, widens definitions beyond basic labels. Add race, gender, or sexual orientation to the mix, and the gaps spread almost impossibly wide.[5] Yet universities and researchers often represent "the veteran" as one class of person, creating significant theoretical and practical tensions.[6]

In fact, differences in service experience make simplistic definitions remarkably ineffectual when universities make decisions in the real world about how best to serve student veterans. While the word *veteran* can be used to identify types of people, the types of services a community might provide to these people and the types of questions researchers might examine surrounding each person's experiences are so broad as to make a single marker of "the veteran experience" utterly reductive and potentially harmful. While the civilian population may see such distinctions as academic or may not even see them at all, we must, if we are to begin to approach veterans studies effectively, begin with the acknowledgment that we frequently erase such distinctions for our convenience or due to our inability (or unwillingness) to wade into the complexity of the issue.

This unwillingness to engage with the complexities of the veteran experience also betrays pervasive essentialist thinking about "the veteran" and the veteran's role in American culture. Such thinking emerges most clearly in portrayals of veterans in popular culture, where one of several tropes dominate representations of "the veteran." The World War II hero, the disenfranchised Vietnam veteran, the violent veteran suffering from PTSD, the veteran who copes with war through drinking or drug abuse, the "healed" veteran who has overcome personal demons, the infallible band of brothers whose loyalty marks a special kinship forged in war—these tropes are noteworthy for several reasons, but perhaps most important is that they, despite their obvious differences, all suggest that one key feature defines a veteran: combat experience.

The fixation on combat, killing, and the violence of war preoccupies not just popular culture, but scholarly inquiry into veterans as well. Studies of risk factors for trauma typically hinge on war violence, and studies of the representations of war in literature, film, art, and media inevitably drift toward representations of combat. Such focus is understandable on a number of fronts. The effects of war violence are far-reaching, and the need to understand and foster action to address them is profound and pressing. Without such scholarship (and often investigative journalism), the casualties of war simply would not be understood. Indeed, many of those casualties would be invisible or forgotten.

This focus on combat as a marker for "veteran-ness" undoubtedly derives from the primary historical purpose of the military: to wage war. The difficult ethical terrain service members face in combat requires attention and, given the United States' ongoing combat operations in foreign lands, discussing the impact of war abroad is necessary for understanding not only the veteran but also American culture more broadly. The work of scholars in peace studies, international conflict, and trauma theory, among many others, helps us rethink the US commitment to warfare and requires us to confront its impact on those we send to fight wars and to "maintain peace" throughout the world. To ignore that aspect of the veteran experience would be to ignore the most ethically charged and pressing of veteran issues.

Nonetheless, the fixation on combat ignores the military experience of the vast majority of military service personnel, and, as a result, obscures other important lines of inquiry. A 2010 Veterans Administration survey found that among veterans of all eras, only 34 percent reported that they had served in a combat or war zone, meaning millions have served in the military without combat experience ("National"). While the number of post-9/11 service members deployed to a war zone is notably higher, at 60 percent (*Military-Civilian Gap*), deployment to a "combat zone" is a technical distinction made by the military that does not readily translate to popular conceptions of overseas deployments. The shifting nature of combat has fundamentally changed what it means to be serving in a combat zone, and many service members who are considered to be "deployed to a war zone" may never see direct combat action. For instance, as of December 2015, the Philippines, Kosovo, and the Adriatic Sea were designated as combat zones due to a presidential executive order, despite no declarations of war by the United States for those areas.

Further, deployment to a war zone does not mean service members have been assigned to direct combat action units or, even more important, that they have ever been engaged in direct combat. Our understanding of the veteran as a combatant, then, fails to take into account vast numbers of service personnel who never actually "fight" in a war.[7] When resources to understand the veteran experience inevitably drift toward the (significant and important) needs of combat veterans, we effectively ignore the needs of a large population within the military demographic. To discuss veterans as primarily combat veterans, then, is not only factually inaccurate, it also constitutes (to invoke Phil Klay and Michael Rothberg) a "failure of the imagination." When we understand "the veteran" as either solely or even primarily a combat veteran, we fail to consider the tremendous diversity within that term.

We hope in this volume to broaden our approaches to studying veterans' experiences, to think more critically about who "the veteran" is and how the term has been constructed (and for what ends). We argue that a more nuanced approach to understanding "the veteran" leads not only to more useful research, but also to more wide-ranging and impactful scholarship and community engagement. More important to the audience of this volume, such an approach leads to more thoughtful engagement with veterans in writing classrooms, where, as we noted earlier, student disclosures are often part and parcel of coursework. In short, we hope to foster greater engagement with those groups of veterans who have been largely ignored without sacrificing necessary attention to combat veterans. Our approach is to identify key areas in research and university initiatives where subtle reorientation might result in significant changes. One of those areas is in university trainings about veterans and their dependents, an area that has been a focus of veterans studies scholarship.

DEFICIT TRAINING, ASSET-BASED INQUIRY, AND THE FOUNDATIONS OF A FIELD

In faculty and staff trainings at many colleges and universities, the focus on combat veterans is pronounced. Indeed, in our discussions with writing faculty, combat and its impact on student veterans is often a primary preoccupation, perhaps in part due to the fact that the great majority of faculty trainings fixate—sometimes exclusively—on recognizing, reporting, and facilitating help for veterans with combat-related PTSD or other mental or physical injuries. Implicit in most of the trainings is the assumption that "the veteran" is not only a combat veteran, but also a male veteran coping with trauma. Among the most frequently used of these trainings are the "Green Zone" training pioneered by Virginia Commonwealth University (whose language, in its invocation of Iraq's ostensibly combat-free Green Zone, implies safety from violence) and the "Got Your Six" training (whose language derives from the military ideal of watching each other's back during a time of imminent danger). Of the forty customizable lecture slides that precede scenario role-plays and discussion in the Green Zone Training provided by VCU, nineteen (or almost half) of the slides emphasize trauma, PTSD, traumatic brain injury (TBI), other "wounds of war," transition difficulties, or disabilities. Therefore, while the intent of these trainings is useful and productive, the impact is one that often serves to perpetuate the notion that a veteran is physically, emotionally, and/or morally wounded[8] or experiencing a constant threat of harm.

We argue in various places throughout this volume that such deficit training models create significant problems for student veterans, their fellow students, and their instructors and advisors, as well as for research inquiries and institutional asset allocations. Because those problems can be significant and create long-lasting legacies within institutions, we advocate for an alternative—an asset-based approach to veterans studies. We detail this approach in the chapters ahead, but we want to emphasize at the outset two key reasons for our insistence upon it. First, this approach requires us—as investigators, proponents, educators, and activists—to challenge institutional conceptions of veterans as well as our own methods of inquiry. As long as institutions focus on veteran deficits and as long as our own research fixates on combat and its repercussions, we cannot reasonably expect cultural dialogue about veterans to diversify. Second, it provides productive points of entry into discussion about veterans' issues without appealing to well-worn stereotypes. When we take an asset-based approach, we engage with the idea of "the veteran" as a category of inherent worth, not in order to glorify military service or elevate veterans above their civilian counterparts (see Moore), nor to erase the complexity of and problems within military institutions, but in order to recognize the veteran identity as one worthy of serious and sustained intellectual engagement regardless of any explicit connection to armed conflict and warfare.

Equally important, this volume advances the idea that writing as an institutional discipline is itself an asset that helps students bridge diverse domains of knowledge. Research on this point continues to expand, and we discuss some of it in detail in the chapters that follow. Nonetheless, we take seriously the classical rhetoric ideal that writing is a heuristic that forms new "ways of knowing and doing" (Carter). Therefore, we articulate in the following pages why we believe writing studies more generally is especially well suited to helping student veterans negotiate their new identities as students as well as encouraging them to draw upon their intersectional identities as veterans. The heart of that reason is the formative nature of writing and the ways that the writing process fosters not only awareness, but also cognitive development for all students. As we will discuss later, some within the military itself are now advocating for writing instruction as part of training for military leaders, a move that, while perhaps unexpected in some respects, reflects growing awareness of the value of advanced literacy.

In the chapters ahead, then, we suggest approaches that unshackle our work from conceptions of veterans as only (male) combat veterans, even while we try to demonstrate the continued need to investigate issues attendant on the combat experience, including trauma and moral injury. At the heart of the former is the idea that greater focus on the transferable assets of "the veteran" helps connect veterans to civilian communities and fosters new inquiry into what it means to have served in the military. At the core of the latter is the idea that even within discourse about trauma, an asset orientation helps us engage more thoughtfully with the wartime experience as, in part, adaptation to impossible circumstances even when we challenge fundamental assumptions about the risks and rewards of being in an occupational field whose mission is to wage war.

We find within this asset approach the foundation of veterans studies as it has grown within the field of writing studies. Veterans studies, as it has been emerging in conferences, scholarship, and curricula, situates itself self-consciously as a field of advocacy for veterans. Indeed, many of the organizations at the front of the field are explicitly oriented toward advocacy, intervention, and outreach. The Veterans Writing Project, spearheaded by Ron Capps, has paired with a variety of organizations in order to aid veteran transition and provide support, launched a journal (*0-Dark Thirty*), and offered writing-to-heal retreats. The Texas Veterans Commission has founded a writing workshop specifically for women veterans called "On Point." In New York City, Brandon Willitts and Matt Gallagher founded Words after War, a writing group that aims to bring together veterans and civilians in cohorts of writers. Words after War has been widely covered in the media and reflects a movement of numerous state- or city-based advocacy groups for veterans to use writing as a means for engaging with and rejoining the civilian population.

Given the extensive focus on public writing and writing for "real" audiences in many of today's composition classes and writing curricula, several writing faculty have found advocacy for veterans to be a natural fit for their classroom work and scholarship. Such advocacy recognizes the strengths of the veteran population even while it acknowledges the challenges it faces, both from within its ranks and from a culture that too easily either glorifies or demonizes it. An asset approach requires us to begin our inquiry into the veteran experience from a place that recognizes that, regardless of the nature, type, or length of service, the moniker "veteran" derives from an intentional training regime and professional ethos that self-consciously aims to transform people from individuals into members of a distinct interdependent community. The complicated nature of that transformation and its potentially problematic results upon an individual's departure from that community must be faced, certainly, but engaging those individuals without first making sense of their purposes and motivations will inevitably lead to misrepresentations and half-truths.

We insist, in other words, that we begin our work with what Peter Elbow famously called the "believing game" in order to ensure that our own first steps are not misinformed or simplistic. This is not to eschew skepticism. Indeed, we will at times argue strenuously for thoughtful skepticism about the idea of "the veteran" and the effects of military service more generally. We assume throughout this introduction to the field, however, that the best scholarship comes from those who consider military service first on its own terms and then demonstrate how we might rethink, problematize, or challenge the cultural forces that foster simplistic narratives about war, veterans, and military families.

A FIELD GUIDE

The rise of veterans studies within WS occurred just as the Conference on College Composition and Communication was recognizing the need for more discussion about veterans. With generous funding from a CCCC Research Initiative Grant, we administered a national survey to collect initial data from WPAs and writing instructors, and over a period of more than eighteen months we traveled the United States interviewing a wide range of stakeholders in student veteran success. We were able to visit more than forty separate institutions,[9] walking campuses, imposing on incredibly gracious faculty, students, staff, and administrators, and tracking down leads not only on college campuses, but off them as well. We interviewed colleagues at conferences, on the phone, and via video conference, and in the years after we first launched this project, we visited even more schools, either separately or together, sometimes by invitation of the institution, other times on a hunch that if we made contact with someone at a particular school, we would uncover yet another innovative approach to addressing the student veteran surge on college campuses. Now having set foot on nearly seventy campuses, we feel we have garnered new insights that, in several instances, changed some of our initial beliefs about what works best for student veterans in the writing classroom, and indeed more generally as well.

In the chapters that follow, we offer in-depth discussion of central concepts that circulate among researchers in veterans studies, especially those that have emerged from scholars in writing studies, and we do so within an easy-to-negotiate framework. We envision each chapter as a starting point into one aspect of veterans studies that is especially important for writing instructors, and we connect each section to relevant research. At the end of each chapter, we offer some "implementation questions" to guide readers as they consider their local contexts and how and whether they might put into practice some of the curricular and institutional changes we discuss. The result is not a "final word" on the field, but instead a clear sense of dominant lines of inquiry and important models of research, pedagogy, and advocacy occurring across the country. Each chapter stands alone as a primer to one aspect of the field, even while the chapters work together to serve as a broader intellectual introduction to the discipline as a whole.

The first two chapters, therefore, provide a historical background on the emergent field of veterans studies by focusing on its genesis among writing faculty after the passage of the current Post-9/11 GI Bill and its effects on writing classrooms and colleges more broadly. While contemporary wars have resulted in a growing veteran population, the most recent iteration of federal educational support for service members is the primary contingency that has launched veterans studies. Without that bill—and without the surging veteran populations on many campuses resulting from it—veterans might well have remained largely invisible to higher education. As student veterans have matriculated, they not only have populated first-year writing courses but have also obliged institutions to consider military service as a feature of their student bodies. Some schools have seen a particularly active student veteran base agitate for change;

others have witnessed advocacy from staff or faculty. In either case, an unexpected outcome of the bill has been the birth of this new field. Understanding the bill and its impact on universities, therefore, is the first part of our study, and we dedicate two chapters to fully exploring its impact not just on universities, but on writing classrooms in particular. While Chapter 1 offers readers a broadbrush sketch of who today's student veterans are and how they may affect campus and classroom culture, Chapter 2 delves into the language of the GI Bill and how it may influence student veterans' expectations and motivations as they enroll at institutions of higher education.

Following Chapter 2, we have placed the first writing/practices interstitial chapter. Here, we provide texts written by student veterans and active military members as well as military writing instructions and guidelines. These materials are meant to provide some concrete examples for our readers to keep in mind and refer back to as we discuss student veterans' prior writing experiences and practices in more detail in subsequent chapters. A second writing/practices interstitial chapter containing military-informed pedagogical materials follows Chapter 5.

In Chapter 3, we draw attention to what student veterans bring intellectually to our institutions within the context of veteran transitions as they are manifested in writing classrooms at two-year and four-year institutions. Within education scholarship on veterans, probably no topic has attracted more attention than veterans' "transition." We survey the research and discuss key findings, but we will also describe a central problem with much of the work: the monolithic status of "the veteran's transition" as a singular moment in the move from the military to the civilian world. We argue that the shift from active service member to veteran is better understood as a process of multiple, complex transitions, many of which are embodied in the writing challenges student veterans face as they move through their education. Because a significant percentage of undergraduate student veterans make a transition from community colleges to traditional four-year institutions, we argue that within higher education we need to consider more carefully the multiple educational transitions student veterans make and the processes that either aid or constrain them. Because writing instruction is typically required at both types of colleges, we emphasize the need for greater understanding of writing pedagogies across these educational settings.

In Chapter 4, we consider more directly specific classroom practices as we discuss the three primary ways that our research has revealed that writing programs are adjusting to veterans in the classroom. Drawing on our findings from the CCCC Research Initiative Grant, we analyze three types of courses that writing faculty have created to address new veteran students in their classrooms. The "veterans-only" classroom limits enrollments solely to veterans or military service members. The "veteran-focused" classroom, while allowing for more open enrollment, self-consciously creates assignments and readings that are focused on issues that may be of interest to veterans. "Veteran-friendly" classrooms are those classrooms in which faculty have been trained to respond to the specific needs of veterans, even if they do not limit class enrollments or try to entice veterans with certain types of course materials or activities. This chapter both theorizes the foundations of these types of courses and details their key features, ultimately arguing that a veteran-friendly course is likely the best choice for most faculty and writing programs.

Finally, we conclude by directly addressing the fixation on trauma within large bodies of research on veterans and describe how faculty and staff trainings focused on a deficit model ultimately distort the impact of veterans on college campuses. We examine trauma theory and disability studies in light of research in writing and suggest they provide cross-disciplinary perspectives through which scholars can approach issues such as PTSD, TBI, and moral injury. The scholarship on writing and trauma is extensive, and our hope is to acknowledge that work while also demonstrating precisely how it applies to veterans in writing classrooms. We further draw attention to the need for a more expansive view of veterans and the problems researchers, professors, and administrators face when combat trauma remains the focus of publications about student veterans.

These aspects of our field's practical and theoretical engagement with veterans (who they are, what they are seeking from higher education, what they bring with them intellectually and practically, what classroom practices they may find most effective, and what the impact of trauma may be), we believe, provide an initial architecture with which faculty and researchers can build new understandings of the interplay between writing studies and veterans studies. Mimicking in some respects the format of a military field manual, we lay out principles and procedures that might animate classroom practices, and we include in the two writing/practices interchapters examples of student writing, samples of military writing, and questions that can help shape a writing program attuned to student veterans. Those practices emerge from theories and research about veterans in writing classrooms. We do not attempt to cover every type of research being conducted, nor do we mean to give the impression that we imagine this volume as the definitive discussion of the thousands of initiatives across the country that address veterans and higher education. It is not, and if our experience visiting communities around the United States has taught us anything, it is that such a summary is simply impossible. The sheer number of people and organizations attempting to attend to veterans' issues, even just those that provide writing opportunities for veterans, is overwhelming. Nonetheless, we hope we provide a useful and clearly conceived description of the primary reasons that veterans studies has emerged and why it has emerged with such force within writing studies. If we are to be faulted for anything, it may be simply that our thoughts about how the field might most productively grow are too personal. They undoubtedly betray certain preferences and prejudices shaped by our own disciplinary backgrounds, scholarly interests, and personal histories. Still, we hope such suggestions are not limiting, but instead productive. We are, indeed, frequently made aware of novel research being conducted across the country that promises innovative new ways of knowing, and it is our sincere hope that this volume, instead of being seen as exclusionary or definitive, will be read as provocative and embracing—of new ideas, of new methods, and of new approaches to understanding the impact of military veterans on our culture and on our campuses.

1

Writing (Veterans) Studies

THE LAST FIFTEEN YEARS HAVE witnessed the birth of a new field of research and pedagogy: veterans studies. The field boasts a national research center at the University of Utah, an international conference ("Veterans in Society"), and multiple regional research and outreach offices at schools such as the University of Missouri–St. Louis (UMSL), the University of Southern California, and Coastal Carolina University. Burgeoning student interest has led to new degree programs across the country, including undergraduate minors at UMSL and Eastern Kentucky University and certificate programs at the University of Southern California and University of Nevada–Reno. Partnerships between university researchers and the Veterans Administration (VA) have emerged to investigate veteran-related issues such as traumatic brain injury (TBI), family planning, and mental-health counseling. In 2014 the National Endowment for the Humanities (NEH) issued a call for projects meant to "encourage humanities programs that focus on the history, experience, or meaning of war and military service" ("NEH Launches"), and an eponymous academic journal published its first issue in 2016. After initially being hosted by Colorado State, the *Journal of Veterans Studies* (*JVS*) has recently moved to Virginia Tech as its publisher and home institution. Virginia Tech also hosted an NEH Summer Institute designed to "serve as a catalyst for building a national, interdisciplinary network of [veterans studies] scholars" (Byron). Increasingly, scholars from multiple disciplines are challenging higher education to prepare for research in the new field (Brodsky and Pencek; Craig; Hicks, Weiss, and Coll; DiRamio), and within numerous academic disciplines, dissertations about veterans, war, and the military have nearly quintupled (Dunbar).

Student Veterans of America (SVA), a long-standing peer-to-peer support organization, has found new purpose and has emerged with significant force not only by growing its presence on campuses, but by providing meaningful research to help advance a national conversation about veterans in higher education. New SVA chapters have increased exponentially, from fewer than 50 before 2010 to 950 in 2014. In fact, membership doubled from 2013 to 2014 alone (Romey). Due to SVA chapters' advocacy as well as other student-driven initiatives on campuses across the country, institutions have bolstered their support for student veterans. Perhaps the most visible support has come in the form of veterans' lounges, with some campuses even committing sufficient resources to build and staff veterans centers, complete with social and recreational activities and support staff who assist with a range of concerns—from benefits processing, academic success, and job placement to counseling and healthcare. Nonprofits such as the Warrior-Scholar Project, the Pat Tillman Foundation, and the Posse Foundation's Veterans Program have explicit missions to aid veterans in their pursuit of educational goals, and a number of colleges and universities sponsor community-based veterans' writing groups, with Syracuse University's (notably launched by faculty members in the rhetoric program there) being among the most long-standing (Schell, "Writing with Veterans" and "Writing the Way Home"; Schell and Kleinbart).

While research from a wide range of groups and academic disciplines has been engaged in considerations of this nascent field of veterans studies, scholars in writing studies have, in many respects, been leading the way in the formation of this new discipline. For example, professionals in the fields of student affairs (Ackerman and DiRamio; Bauman; DiRamio and Jarvis; Coll and Weiss; Canfield and Weiss; Vaccaro) and higher education administration (Rumann and Hamrick; Zinger and Cohen; Vacchi; Vacchi and Berger; Bonar and Domenici) have provided important contributions to current understandings of veterans in higher education, but their work is typically focused on either student services for veterans or discussions of trauma and mental health. In contrast, scholars in WS have extended the field beyond those two considerations, providing more detailed and nuanced discussions of veterans as a student population while also theorizing the significance of student veterans to campus learning communities.

For example, writing studies' largest professional organization, the Conference on College Composition and Communication (CCCC), has been deeply engaged in practical and theoretical discussions related to student veterans. In 2009 the Writing with Current, Former, and Future Members of the Military Special Interest Group met for the first time at the CCCC Annual Convention (the group was awarded standing group status in 2015). The following year, in 2010, Marilyn Valentino used her chair's address to acknowledge the rapidly growing demographic of Iraq and Afghanistan war veterans entering first-year writing classes. Valentino's comments ended with the assertion that those of us within the discipline "have an ethical obligation to react responsibly" to veterans in our classrooms. Valentino's remarks challenged writing instructors to consider the changing demographics of students when crafting assignments and offering support to student writers. It has been a challenge that a sizable cohort of teachers, scholars, and administrators in WS have taken to heart. In December 2011, under the direction of Gwen Pough, CCCC appointed a Task Force on Student Veterans, whose primary charge was to compose a position statement on student veterans in the college composition classroom; the document, "Student Veterans in the College Composition Classroom: Realizing Their Strengths and Assessing Their Needs," was published on the CCCC website in 2015.

The field's journals have supported these conversations, as well. In 2009, the same year that the Special Interest Group convened at the CCCC Convention, *Teaching English in the Two-Year College* (*TETYC*) published a special issue containing "essays [that] contemplate complicated teaching moments because they acknowledge that our military veterans cannot be defined entirely by their identities as soldiers; their lives before and after military service are much richer and broader than that single identity. Indeed, so are the lives of their instructors" (S[ommers] 338). The following year, *Kairos* published a special issue focused on rhetoric, technology, and the military; a special issue of *Composition Forum* focused on veterans and writing was released in 2013; and a special issue of *Reflections: Public Writing, Civic Rhetoric, and Service Learning* dedicated to veterans' writing appeared in 2016. The *Journal of Veterans Studies* (*JVS*) was conceived of and launched by writing studies scholar Mariana Grohowski in 2016. Many of the members of the *JVS* editorial board as well as those who have published in the journal are also writing studies scholars. Also of note, Sue Doe and Lisa Langstraat's influential edited collection *Generation Vet: Composition, Student-Veterans, and the Post-9/11 University* was published in 2014.

In addition to these organizational efforts and scholarly publications, we want to draw attention to two developments in WS that have been especially important for the growth of veterans studies in our field. First, writing faculty are often on the proverbial "frontlines" of veterans' transitions to higher education. As we have already briefly discussed, this unique positionality is largely a result of the general-education requirements that mandate that all students take first-year writing courses—and often upper-level writing courses as well. Valentino's assertion that writing instructors have ethical obligations to student veterans derives from this insight, and scholars such as Linda S. De La Ysla theorize composition faculty as "first responders" as a result of this institutional fact. Indeed, throughout the growing body of research on veterans in the classroom is the recognition that first-year writing in particular is often the place of "first contact," where veterans are oriented to university expectations and support systems through acts of writing and meaningful engagement with faculty and classmates.

Second, writing scholars continue to expand notions of "the veteran" to include frequently ignored populations. While combat veteran trauma continues to be the focus of scholarship in many other fields, among them psychology, sociology, and higher education policy, researchers in WS have broadened approaches to include noncombat veterans of various races, genders, and ethnicities. Certainly, examination of trauma remains important to WS investigators, but in the face of increasingly nuanced exploration of the student veteran community by WS scholars, the trauma focus has given way to broader concerns. This expanded notion undoubtedly comes from the fact that writing faculty encounter far more students in their classrooms who broaden their vision of who constitutes a "student veteran" than those working solely with more specialized student groups, whether they be those studying discrete concepts in psychology or those researching the impact of trauma on cognitive performance within more specialized learning environments. Writing faculty, in other words, tend to teach more and more varied student veterans than most other faculty and therefore experience a fuller range of student veteran performance. That range has led to a more expansive consideration of the student veteran population.

Indeed, the expansiveness of writing faculty's engagement with student veterans leads to stronger grounding in the realities of student veterans as a body of learners, realities that almost inevitably point to their successes more than their failures. The result is that WS scholars have complicated the vision of the veteran and have challenged well-entrenched stereotypes that other scholarship sometimes unwittingly perpetuates. If other fields have fixated on the necessary and important work of understanding student veteran trauma, WS has focused on the equally important work of addressing the veteran as a member of a student body demographic with already diverse needs and expectations, a move that in some ways more accurately represents how faculty are likely to encounter the veteran experience in their classrooms. WS research has therefore functioned as a corrective to well-worn tropes that undermine more thoughtful engagement with student veterans, thus bringing into clearer focus the diversity of the student body within any particular classroom.

In addition to those two major impacts, scholarship from WS more broadly has provided insight into the intersection of contemporary cultural theories and the literacy practices of veterans,

extended examinations of trauma and writing, and broadened discussions of issues of gender, agency, and written expression (Leonhardy; Valentino, "CCCC Chair's Address" and "Serving"; Martin;
Corley; Hart and Thompson, "Ethical," "War," and "Veterans";
Weisser, Ballif, Hart, and Thompson; Crawley; Doe and Langstraat; Grohowski; Blaauw-Hara, "Military" and "Learning"; Hembrough). That a large number of the prime movers in the formation
of veterans studies are trained in rhetoric, composition, writing,
and communication suggests that our field offers, in some way, a
more coherent—even if not exhaustive—framing of the emergence
of veterans studies than is available to other fields. Yet despite the
impressive amount of research regarding veterans that has been
produced by writing studies teacher-scholars in the last decade,[1]
the nature of veterans studies as a field has yet to be surveyed in
any systematic way, and this volume is an attempt to fill that void.

In what follows, we identify some of the primary exigencies that
have led to the development of veterans studies as a scholarly discipline, and we examine the nature of its modes of inquiry, its practices and pedagogies, and its prospects going forward. Again, while
not an exhaustive survey of the discipline, this volume nonetheless
offers scholars, students, and advocates a foundation in the field as
well as new insights into the relationships between veterans studies
and, primarily, writing studies. Like many other expansive fields
of study, such as women's, gender, and sexuality studies (Crowley),
black studies (Aldridge and Young; Rojas), Latinx studies (Flores),
and refugee studies (Black), veterans studies productively reaches
across traditional academic disciplines, finds proponents within
many types of campus departments and organizations, and intentionally engages with communities outside the halls of academe.

As Glenn Phillips and Yvonna Lincoln note, "Tracing the history of critical theories suggests a chronology of underserved student populations in higher education . . . [and the] new population
of students that deserves both researcher and practitioner attention
is student veterans" (658). This attention has come from schools
of education, business and entrepreneurship, and social work, as
well as disciplines such as disability studies, history, cultural theory,

literary studies, fine arts, higher education administration, student affairs, counseling, and many others. All enjoy vibrant cohorts of scholars, educators, and students engaging with veterans' issues. Within this conspicuous, yet dispersed, development of programs, courses, and scholarly research comes a need to delineate central questions and dominant lines of inquiry animating the field. Therefore, this volume provides an initial, dynamic framework for that inquiry, especially in terms that relate to scholars and teachers of writing.

VETERANS AND WRITING STUDIES: GUIDING PRINCIPLES

Rather than offer a narrow set of practices or definitions that cannot possibly fit all contexts, we in this chapter offer some guiding principles that we believe can help shape institutional responses to each reader's particular circumstances. These principles are grounded in contemporary research on US military veterans, especially as it relates to higher education. After providing the theoretical framework, we end this chapter and those that follow with a set of related implementation questions to assist readers as they begin and/or extend conversations and programs on their own campuses. Then, primarily through our writing/practices interchapters, we provide specific examples that illustrate how and why particular responses may work for particular exigencies or why they may not. Those examples are drawn from our survey data, semistructured interviews, informal conversations with colleagues and other stakeholders, and secondary research, and we attempt, where relevant, to include examples drawn directly from active service members, veterans, military family members, faculty, and students who have negotiated, in some form or fashion, the domain we now label "veterans studies."

Principle 1: Veteran Demographics Affect Campus Culture and Writing Classrooms

The rapid growth of both veterans and active duty military on college campuses since 9/11 has been the subject of numerous studies (Ackerman and DiRamio; Rumann and Hamrick; Steele, Salcedo, and Coley; DiRamio and Jarvis; Radford; Livingston et al.; McBain et al.; Vacchi and Berger; Moore). These studies confirm that many institutions of higher education have seen a dramatic rise in the number of service members (past and present) who are enrolled in their courses and programs—primarily at the undergraduate level. More important, writing programs have been on the proverbial "frontline" of the influx of veterans to campuses. The result has been an active response to veterans by writing teachers, students, and scholars (see, for instance, the works of Leonhardy; Valentino; Doe and Langstraat; Hart and Thompson; Blaauw-Hara; Hembrough; Skinnell; and Wilson and Wright).

The nature of the increase in student veterans in writing classrooms, however, varies considerably. The diversity of the US military has been the subject of extensive commentary, especially in the years just after the onset of Operation Enduring Freedom (OEF) and Operation Iraqi Freedom (OIF), when military recruiting tactics came under considerable scrutiny for "predatory" recruitment activities (Bronner; McCormick; Harding and Kershner; Linehan). In 2016, "minority veterans made up about 22 percent of the total veteran population," with "the two largest minority veteran groups [being] Black or African American (11 percent) and Hispanic (7 percent)" (National Center for Veterans Analysis and Statistics [NCVAS], *Profile of Veterans*). Although such diversity exists within the veteran population, and while the Department of Defense embraces the idea that military service is a source of social integration (Keller), a significant percentage of active service members and veterans continue to be white men, which often leads to overgeneralizations. For example, the expansion of service opportunities for women in the United States Armed Forces means that the most commonly held stereotype of "the veteran" as a white male combat survivor is out of touch with the realities of the OIF/OEF student veteran population. Although women make up only 9 percent of all veterans, "a higher percent of women veterans have higher education attainment and are enrolled in higher education compared to men veterans"; in addition, "a higher percent of female veterans are racially and ethnically diverse than male veterans" (NCVAS, *Profile of Women Veterans*).

Indeed, the complex history of women in the US military has been widely discussed (Klein; Solaro; McLagan and Sommers; Benedict; Mulhall; Monahan and Neidel-Greenlee; Biank; Harris, Sumner, and González-Prats; Baechtold and De Sawal; Eichler; Grohowski and Hart), and several core lessons stand out with particular force when colleges and universities consider how to address veteran needs on campus. First, female veterans consistently report that people (including their educators and classmates) are "surprised" to learn they are veterans (Kato et al. 9), and when they do identify as such, they typically find that "their service is misunderstood or discounted" (Santovec, "Women Veterans" 29). To complicate matters further, "women veterans [often] fail to self-identify" (Blanton and Foster 25), in part because they themselves often "don't think of themselves as 'veterans'" (Santovec, "Women Veterans" 29). In addition, as Florence Hamrick and Corey Rumann point out, "studies suggest that women are disproportionately affected by particular experiences in the military, and colleges and universities should be aware of the potential implications for women veterans and servicemembers who subsequently enroll in college" (1). One of the most relevant implications is that women veterans are "less likely to benefit from the camaraderie and social support of [their military] unit, due to power and control issues that men don't face"; as a result, "[m]any female veterans don't want to meet with, much less hang out with, their male peers" (Santovec, "Women Vets" 2), which is likely to cause them to feel even more isolated on college campuses. It may also have an impact on their willingness to work alongside male veterans in a peer-review group or collaborative writing project.

The change in recent years from the "Don't Ask, Don't Tell" (DADT) policy (10 U.S.C. 654) has had an impact on the diversity of the veteran population as well. From 1993 until September 20, 2011, the Department of Defense abided by the DADT policy that effectively allowed gays and lesbians to serve in the military as long as their sexuality remained a secret.[2] For the full duration of OIF and most of OEF, in other words, LGB service members could serve only if their sexual identities were either erased or subsumed under the "higher calling" of a military identity. According to a study by the Williams Institute in 2010, "lifting DADT restrictions [had the potential to] attract [more] men and women to active duty service" (Gates); however, a study conducted one year after the repeal of DADT found that the "preponderance of evidence suggests that repeal has not had any discernible impact, either positive or negative, on recruitment or retention" (Belkin et al. 592). In 2016, five years after the repeal, "nearly 71,000 (2.8%) military personnel across all the services identif[ied] as lesbian, gay, or bisexual" (Goldbach and Castro 1). Yet, like women veterans, LGB veterans may not have experienced the same depth of camaraderie in their military units as heterosexual veterans, which is likely to affect their interactions with other student veterans on campus and their decisions about whether to identify as veterans or not.

While the repeal of DADT did not lift prohibitions against transgender service members, on June 30, 2016, Secretary of Defense Ash Carter released DTM 16-005, which announced a new policy allowing open service by transgender individuals. Prior to the release of DTM 16-005, researchers at the Williams Institute conducted a study that estimated that "21.4% of transgender individuals have served in the military," which, given that "approximately 10.7% of adults in the U.S." have served in the military, suggests that "transgender individuals are about twice as likely as [other] adults in the U.S. to have served their country in the armed forces" (Gates and Herman 3–4). A 2016 survey by the Student Veterans of America (SVA) found that 4.88 percent of student veteran respondents identified as LGBT (Cate). However, as David Vacchi and Joseph Berger point out, "No matter what the exact percentage of GLBT student veterans is, realizing that GLBT student veterans are likely one of the least acknowledged populations on any given campus is critical" (110). Writing programs, therefore, may want to collaborate with diversity offices and LGBT centers and student groups on campus to increase the recognition and support of LGBT student veterans.

A more visible and commonly discussed issue is the range of disability among combat veterans. The prevalence of media stories reporting on the "signature wounds"—Traumatic Brain Injury (TBI) and Post-Traumatic Stress Disorder (PTSD)—of the post-9/11 Global War on Terror (GWoT) has had an especially powerful impact on popular narratives about veterans of the current era, leading to broad claims about the nature of both military experience and veterans that, while important, may misrepresent the extent of the issue—especially for educators. As Vacchi and Berger make clear, "The most important aspect for higher education professionals to keep in mind is that the incidence of TBI and the more familiar post-traumatic stress disorder (PTSD) is low as a percentage of the overall military and veteran population. . . . [A]vailable statistics conclusively suggest that most colleges and universities should not have a heavy burden of serving severely traumatized or wounded veterans" (111). While educators should absolutely make available the necessary support for those student veterans who have been traumatized or wounded during their service, the default assumption should not be that student veterans will require accommodations. We discuss this more in Chapter 5.

Principle 2: Veterans Are Writers
Driving a portion of this study is the idea that many veterans, whether they fully appreciate it or readily acknowledge it or not, enter writing classrooms with significant experience as professional writers. Many veterans have written extensively in their military jobs, and many have even received formal instruction in writing genres that are specific to the military. As Nicholas Osborne points out, "[b]efore pursuing a degree many veterans have mastered foreign languages, worked with foreign governments, operated and maintained expensive and high-tech equipment, managed others, performed life-saving medical duties, and applied critical leadership and decision-making skills in tense situations" (248). The result is that many veterans who enter undergraduate writing classrooms have real-world, concrete experience with professional writing genres, some of which were especially high stakes. These high-stakes genres may range from those linked to combat (such as military briefs presented before combat action), to safety inspections for equipment or records for inventories, to routine corre-

spondence (meeting minutes, memos, letters, vendor contracts), to performance reviews or promotions. Some military writing is linked to basic issues of logistics and operational activities, and some to citations for medals or other awards. Some veterans write speeches for senior officers, some produce documents for distribution to the civilian media, and others write the equivalent of requests for proposals (RFPs), after-action reviews (AARs), or textbooks. (We include and discuss some examples of military writing genres in the writing/practices interchapters.) Others compose poems, fiction, or song lyrics. Almost all consistently write to family and loved ones, whether in print or electronically. Many keep personal journals. Clearly, the range of writing and the volume of documents produced by members of the armed services is staggering, and it varies from one military branch to another, from rank to rank, and from individual to individual.

The variety of writing tasks and experiences within the military leads to considerable complexity in student veteran writing histories. Indeed, branches of service establish writing standards and styles in which service members are expected to write. For example, the Army writing style is highly standardized in order to ensure clear communication. The US Army Combined Arms Center provides a primer for that style in their training for Warrant Officers. The Army standard is stated as "transmits a clear message in a single rapid reading and is generally free of errors in grammar, mechanics, and usage." A general summary of the Army writing style is below:

1. Put the recommendation, conclusion or reason for writing—the bottom line—in the first or second paragraph, not at the end.
2. Use the active voice.
3. Use short sentences (an average of 15 or fewer words).
4. Use short words (three syllables or fewer).
5. Write paragraphs that average 6 to 7 sentences in length.
6. Use correct spelling, grammar, and punctuation.
7. Use "I," "you," and "we" as subjects of sentences instead of "this office," "this headquarters," "all individuals," and so forth for most kinds of writing.

8. Retype correspondence only when pen and ink changes are not allowed, when the changes make the final product look sloppy, or when the correspondence is going outside DA [Direct Action] or to the general public. In general, do not retype correspondence to make minor corrections.

Because writing is highly controlled and stylized within the military even as document genres vary between service branches (a set of executable orders or a preventative maintenance report written by an Air Force veteran may be appreciably different from those written by a Coast Guard veteran, for example), student veterans may enter the writing classroom with diverse, if not outright contradictory, understandings of what constitutes effectiveness for certain genres of military writing, not to mention limited understandings of the conventions of college-level academic writing genres and citation practices. Further, because audience is typically standardized or embedded within the military hierarchy, the idea of writing to diverse (often imagined) audiences may be especially challenging even as the idea of writing with clear purpose and concrete, actionable outcomes is not.

Regardless of a student veteran's military rank, rate, and time in service, however, writing instructors and writing program administrators (WPAs) will benefit from understanding that many veterans will enter their classrooms with considerable high-stakes writing experiences that have real audiences and significant, often immediate, impact. As Corrine Hinton explains, "two types of prior knowledge—of general discourse forms and of domain specific topics—are important to consider as we learn about the prior knowledge many student veterans bring with them into their composition classrooms" ("Military"). When writing faculty and/or academic advisors assume "that all veterans [have] been 'away' from writing so long that they [need] a basic refresher course" (Vaccaro 352), it is understandably insulting and potentially alienating for student veterans. In fact, the 2016 SVA survey found that 60 percent of student veteran respondents indicated that they found their college writing courses to be "extremely easy, very easy, or easy" (Cate). However, even if student veterans consider themselves to be proficient professional writers, their military writing experiences and the documents that emerged from them (several of which we feature in the writing/practices interchapters) will likely bear little resemblance to the types of academic writing genres so many writing programs and faculty expect students to produce; and given the high stakes and/or directly actionable nature of most military writing, the point or purpose of academic genres may not be readily apparent to student veterans either. Student veterans are also likely to expect direct markings or corrections (see "pen and ink changes" above) to be made to their written work by their teacher (their "direct report").

The result is that faculty will likely need to focus on helping student veterans transfer aspects of their previous writing experiences to an academic setting. The writing challenges student veterans experience primarily emerge from their relative fluency in genres and styles of writing for which first-year writing faculty have little or no context, for instance, the use of sentence fragments and bulleted lists or the convention of producing "texts that are often recycled, repurposed, and appropriated without the need for individual authorial attribution" (Anson and Neely). In such instances, faculty may misread a student veteran's writing habits as deficits needing correction instead of negotiations of genre conventions and may miss an opportunity to discuss aspects of rhetorical contexts that can facilitate the writer's success.

Such an approach is in line with research on writing transfer, which recognizes that "[w]riters consistently draw on prior knowledge in order to navigate within and among various contexts for writing and learning," but the challenge for writers and their instructors is "bringing what [the writers] know to conscious attention in order to think about similarities and differences between what [they] know and have done and what [they] must do now" (Anson and Moore 7).

Accordingly, we echo Doug Brent, who points out that "the idea that rhetorical genres are deeply bound with particular exigencies seriously complicates the question of transfer from one setting to another" (399), and therefore "it is important to provide explicit cues that encourage learners to consider the relation between the source and target of transfer" (413). While Brent identifies the source of genre knowledge as the classroom and the target of transfer as the workplace, student veteran writers will be attempting to transfer their knowledge in the opposite direction. As Hinton makes clear, a student veteran "who believes that his or her prior knowledge is valuable to current contexts is more likely to use those experiences or knowledge in the building of new knowledge *but generally only when prompted or guided to do so*" (emphasis added). Consequently, writing faculty must recognize that they have an "important role . . . in creating a learning environment where student veterans can feel comfortable enough to share or not share their experiences and also in respecting the value of these experiences and perceptions even if they make us uncomfortable or challenge our perceptions of writing or of higher education" (Hinton, "Military"). In other words, while writing faculty can reasonably expect student veterans to learn and apply the conventions of academic discourse, student veterans should likewise be able to reasonably expect their faculty members to respect the influence of their previous experiences— with writing and beyond.

Principle 3: Not All Institutions or Writing Programs Need a Systemic Response to Student Veterans

Investment in helping student veterans often yields considerable positive results, but at a time when many institutions are facing financial hardship, allocating resources for student veteran support or faculty training may not be viable. While some institutions have large and growing veteran populations on their campuses, others have virtually none. Although we would argue that any sort of institutional support for student veterans is desirable and, indeed, likely transferable to other student populations, we are not suggesting that all institutions or programs need to invest in training or allocate significant resources to facilitate student veteran success. Many universities see veteran populations cycle through boom and bust enrollments, and others, especially many small private liberal arts colleges (see Sloane, "Veterans" and "Annual"), have a very small percentage of student veterans on campus. In those instances, institutional resources may be more productively used for other or shared resources (e.g., affiliation with other identity groups and/or support services such as adult students, commuters, first-generation students, diversity and inclusion centers, etc.). In sum, we want to emphasize that not all schools need to inquire further into their student veteran population, even as we also insist that for those schools with large student veteran populations, the writing faculty need to understand and engage with that demographic as distinctive.

(For a complete heuristic to guide an initial assessment of veteran populations, writing assets/needs, and interdisciplinary programmatic support, see Writing/Practices 2.)

CONCLUSION

Veteran populations within classrooms are often invisible to instructors. There is no universal veteran "tell" that instructors can read to discern if veterans are populating a classroom. Even if some student veterans speak openly about their service or carry items or wear clothing that demonstrates pride in their military life, others will move into colleges and intentionally seek to leave that part of their lives behind, effectively making it impossible for faculty to know about their prior service. In fact, many student veterans may consciously choose to be "stealth veterans": "A stealth veteran is a veteran who does not identify as such in the classroom because he or she does not want to be objectified as a veteran, be perceived somehow as less than whole, or be requested to tell war stories" (Handley 108). For that reason, even if WPAs do not think they have sizable veteran populations on their campuses, we recommend at the very least connecting with the Certifying Official and/or Veteran Service Officer to seek answers to some of the generative questions included in the heuristic in our Writing/Practices 2. The results may be surprising and may warrant a focused, intentional response.

Chapter 1 Implementation Questions

- What are the demographics of the veterans on your campus?
- Are veterans from certain service branches more likely to be at your campus than others?
- Does your campus have an active student veteran organization?
- How many veterans are taking classes in person or online at your institution?
- Are veterans taking writing courses at your campus or transferring them in from another institution?
- Do your writing courses provide opportunities for veterans to explore the rhetorical aspects of the types of writing they used in the service?

2

The Rhetoric of the GI Bill: Defining Veteran Education

IN A PREAMBLE TO THE Post-9/11 GI Bill, the US Veterans Administration provides a brief history of previous GI bills and their relevance to the development of American culture after World War II. While this brief history predictably lauds the various GI bills of the last seventy years, it also signals that support for governmental—and taxpayer—subsidy of veteran education has hardly been a universally praised concept. The history recounts the near failures of the first major bill, the Servicemen's Readjustment Act of 1944, and the changes it underwent in order to eventually become law. It also, as a lead-up to a discussion in praise of the Post-9/11 GI Bill,[1] presents the Montgomery GI Bill of the post–Vietnam era as an updating of earlier iterations of the original bill. Indeed, what is striking in the discussion is the degree to which the preamble focuses on the tensions surrounding the 1944 act and its eventual triumph. Those tensions resonate today:

> Some shunned the idea of paying unemployed veterans $20 a week because they thought it diminished their incentive to look for work. Others questioned the concept of sending battle-hardened veterans to colleges and universities, a privilege then reserved for the rich. Despite their differences, all agreed something must be done to help veterans assimilate into civilian life. (*Born*)

The concerns here about whether veterans, as a particular class of Americans, deserved special considerations from the federal government would recur with each new GI bill and its amendments, yet the argument that eventually seems to win the day is that veterans, because of their military service, deserve benefits not accorded to other US citizens. While such an idea is embraced by many in contemporary America, the support is hardly universal when it comes to actually funding the GI Bill's mandate. Intense arguments have raged in Congress, and the result has been ongoing debates about the nature of military service today and the obligations of a government to those who have chosen to serve in a time of an all-volunteer force as well as the type of education that will be authorized.

Similarly intense debates within colleges and universities about the relationship between military service and the goals of higher education have also emerged.[2] Henry Giroux, for example, has been an ardent critic of what he terms "the militarization" of higher education. According to Giroux, "the post-9/11 resurgence of patriotic commitment and support on the part of faculty and administrators towards the increasing militarization of daily life runs the risk of situating academia within a larger project in which the militarized narratives, values and pedagogical practices of the warfare state become commonplace" (58). In order to prevent militarization from becoming "a powerful pedagogical force that shapes our lives, memories and daily experiences, while erasing everything critical and emancipatory about history, justice, solidarity and the meaning of democracy," he argues, "higher education [must] be defended as a vital public sphere crucial for both the education of critical citizens and the defense of democratic values and institutions" (58).[3] Such categorizations of military service can lead to the perception that the goals of a liberal arts education, in particular, are at odds with military educational agendas. The military's hierarchized rank system and training for violence can lead to the superficial conclusion that military service requires service members to abdicate core features of a liberal education, among them critical thinking and questioning and a commitment to human rights. Such perceptions, grounded in popular conceptions about the armed services, rarely connect to stated military objectives, which frequently include extensive training in problem solving and discussion around ambiguity and the nature of human motivation. Concerns about the nature of military training that position a liberal education as contrary or oppositional to the military are typically based upon extreme examples that fail to consult actual military training guidelines or educational practices.

Critiques like those of Giroux often have at their core a static definition of "the veteran" or "service member" that is, even if historically accurate, remarkably disconnected from the demographics of veterans today. The types of people who serve within the American military have changed dramatically over the last century, with the armed services in some cases diversifying its officer and enlisted ranks more rapidly than many university faculty and student populations. These changes were accompanied by military guidance and instruction grounded in diversity.

While the original GI Bill focused almost exclusively on male veterans, it did so largely due to military limitations on who could serve and who was drafted. Women were not (and are still not) required to register for the draft ("Women and the Draft"), and the proportion of male service members in World War II topped 97 percent. In addition, during the Second World War women in the US military were considered to be serving in "auxiliary" or "temporary" status and were typically discharged immediately when the fighting ended (Holm 128–29). Therefore, while the language of the 1944 bill indicates that "any person who served in the active military or naval service on or after September 16, 1940" and prior to the termination of the war was eligible for GI Bill benefits, these benefits were enjoyed almost exclusively by male veterans.

According to research published by the City University of New York (CUNY), only 2.9 percent of eligible World War II female veterans "attended college on the G.I. Bill. Many women did not know they were eligible and post-war culture and social policy encouraged and/or forced women out of the workplace, stressing their roles as homemakers, wives, and mothers" (*Investing*). With the Post-9/11 GI Bill, however, demographics have changed considerably. In 2015, women made up 16.8 percent of the active duty forces ("2015 Demographics" 6), more than five times greater than the percentage of women serving in World War II. In addition, as we noted previously, although women make up only 9 percent of all current veterans, "a higher percent of women veterans have higher education attainment and are enrolled in higher education compared to men veterans" (NCVAS, *Profile of Women Veterans*).

Like women, minority service members in World War II were also accorded a different status than that of white men. Not only did "African American servicemen [have] to serve in a segregated Army and Navy while they fought for democracy overseas," but "when black World War Two veterans in Georgia, Alabama, and Mississippi tried to use the GI Bill to improve their socio-economic conditions, they could not do so because of a combination of racial discrimination and the poor administration of the bill's benefits" (Onkst 518).[4] While today's military is no longer segregated, and "Black or African American members represent 17.0 percent" ("2015 Demographics" 7) of the total military force, disparities remain, as evidenced by the fact that "Black returning vets are utilizing GI benefits less than other ethnic groups" (Ottley 80).

Another difference between the original bill and the current bill relates to benefits accorded to physically disabled veterans.[5] In 1944,

> [t]he roughly 1.6 million disabled veterans of the war fell under a different law, Public Law 16, whose provisions placed them in a separate category defined by dependence. . . . Unlike the G.I. Bill, Public Law 16 emphasized vocational rehabilitation and a quick reentry into the labor market. Disabled veterans who wanted to earn a college degree, rather than vocational training, faced significant obstacles. (Rose 26)

Fortunately, due in part to the passage of the Americans with Disabilities Act (ADA) in 1990 and the ADA Amendments Act of 2008, university administrators are less likely to be "unfamiliar and fearful of people with disabilities" or "convinced that disabled students—especially those with mobility impairments or who [use] wheelchairs—[do] not belong on college campuses" (Rose 26).

Despite these notable demographic shifts within the military forces and changes within the larger American society and within higher education itself, the federal government has essentially kept the definition of the veteran the same: a person who has completed their term of military service and has been honorably discharged, or has separated from service due to an acceptable medical discharge. The current official definition is "any person who served in the active military, naval, or air service, and who was discharged or released therefrom under conditions other than dishonorable" (38 C.F.R. §3.203), even though, as a congressional white paper indicates, "not all types of service are considered active military service for this purpose" (Szymendera 1–2), noting that in some instances, those in the reserve component may not be considered active duty.

In 1944 the definition, as it applied to those seeking educational benefits, was virtually identical: "any person who served in the active military or naval service on or after September 16, 1940, and prior to the termination of the present war, and who shall have been discharged or released therefrom under conditions other than dishonorable, and who either shall have served ninety days or more . . . or shall have been discharged or released from active service by reason of an actual service-incurred injury or disability." The consistency of the definition over time points to how well-entrenched portions of the GI Bill have become. Again, despite significant differences over time in the types of people securing veteran status as a result of significant demographic changes within the military, the actual definition of a "veteran" has hardly changed.

Such an observation is more than academic. In terms of implementation for educational rights in particular, it points to a remarkably resilient definition, one capable of either accreting or shedding different people under its purview, and, in the case of the military, it suggests a capacity for rapid change. That is, despite the stability of the definition of *veteran* in official documents, the term retains flexibility that is then deployed to various sectors with remarkable speed and agility. When such deployment occurs (and the metaphor here is purposeful), institutions that accept veterans through benefits afforded them by law must be able to respond with similar flexibility and speed. The issue, of course, is that they often cannot.

For educational benefits, this phenomenon of the changing nature of the veteran (despite the defined person of "the veteran" remaining stable) is especially noteworthy. While colleges and universities may have integrated (white, male, able-bodied) veterans in a large scale in the 1940s and 1950s, that integration hardly changed the overall demographic of universities of that time, which remained primarily populated by white, male, able-bodied middle-class students. As veterans have changed, however, their needs have changed along with them, and universities, especially state schools that have witnessed historical drawdowns of state funding, have often struggled to provide sufficient services to their increasingly diverse student bodies. Veteran populations have only added to that diversity; as a result, veterans' fuller integration onto college campuses requires greater resources than many universities are able to provide. Put another way, just at the moment that the military has released a historically diverse group of veterans into the higher education system, that system, established for decades under a more uniform and historically homogenous vision of "the veteran," has collapsed, unable to fund a meaningful response to the wide range of student academic preparedness, background, mental and physical well-being, and socioeconomic status that now constitute the same category of student. For example, developmental writing and mathematics courses that do not count toward graduation requirements are not covered by GI Bill benefits.

CODIFYING VETERAN EDUCATION AS EMPLOYMENT

The resulting lapses in support point to a codification of "the veteran" that remains on many college campuses and one that, in fact, fails to recognize the expansive range of people who now choose military careers—especially in light of the fact that 75 percent of those who enlist in the military claim that receiving education benefits is a primary motivation driving that decision (*Military-Civilian Gap* 33). This demographic range requires special consideration, and while the less-than-nimble response from institutions of higher education should be read historically as derived from a previously more predictable type of incoming student (and veteran), it also should be read as a response to a parallel codification of educational outcomes written into the GI bills that has undermined a wider range of possibilities for veterans within higher education. Indeed, veteran education itself has been codified since the inception of the 1944 GI Bill in ways that limit greater veteran educational opportunities, and such limitations have only put universities under increased strain to respond to the needs of service members.

The context of the first GI Bill established a precedent in the goals of veteran postmilitary education funding that has persisted despite significant changes to student demographics and the sociopolitical and cultural changes to service in the US Armed Forces over the last seventy years. The primary contingency that gave rise to the 1944 GI Bill was the perceived need to advance an economic agenda that was in no small part derived from anxiety about the economic stability of postwar America. As the VA's preamble summarizes it, the Servicemen's Readjustment Act of 1944 "was seen as a genuine attempt to thwart a looming social and economic crisis. Some saw inaction as invitation to another depression" ("History"). With thousands of personnel returning from foreign duty and with a labor force decimated by a persistent and expansive global war, many economists and policymakers worried publicly about the viability of the United States' industrial engine. Military spending in the years just after the war dropped by nearly 90 percent (Higgs 8), much of that due to the release of veterans into the civilian workforce. But, without the proverbial war machine, employment was a primary concern of not only the veterans themselves, but the United States Congress as well.

As a result, many saw the returning (male) veteran as a vehicle for industrial and commercial productivity. Certainly, many policymakers lauded the return of "heroes" and their victories abroad against tyranny, but such adulation ran alongside genuine fear that without a war machine driving economic growth, many working-age men would be left without jobs and without pathways to find new work. That the GI Bill provided for especially attractive home loans and a simple base pay testifies to this anxiety in perhaps the clearest way, but the incentive to send veterans to college campuses was no less driven by the desire to ensure vocational successes and productivity. As a result, the higher education portion of the original GI Bill emphasized, albeit sometimes only tacitly, the need for veterans to study toward gainful employment.[6] Higher education was imagined, in other words, as workplace training.

Such conceptualization was decidedly uncharacteristic for some segments of the American public, especially the upper-middle and upper classes. Like Giroux, those groups embraced the liberal arts ideal of a well-rounded individual whose place was to advance common culture and civic life (indeed, often "civility" itself), a place that presumed a certain socioeconomic stability and cultural capital as footing from which to grow. For those populations, the university as vocational training was relegated to traditional spheres like law, the clergy, or medicine, and they embarked on educational agendas largely unchanged since before the wars. For the military, however, education was, at root, about training for specific jobs, and so it should come as no surprise that policies seeking to ensure veterans maintained their livelihoods moved in that direction. It was both part of military culture writ large, and also the expectation of many of the enlisted personnel, who while in service received different kinds of trainings aimed directly at very specific jobs and duties. For many of the recipients of the GI Bill, to be educated was, as it remains today, a pathway to financial independence and civic participation, regardless of socioeconomic background.[7]

Contemporary discussions about the rise of the so-called "corporate university" often fail to recognize the broad and deep roots of a vocational training model of education embedded within the 1944 GI Bill or its far-reaching effects. For example, this recognition is absent from James A. Côté and Anton Allahar's history of the rise of the "pseudo-vocational" university in their widely reviewed book on "the rise of the corporate university." Similarly, the connection between postwar American anxieties about finding veterans employment does not make a mark in the once-lauded paean to liberal education by Henry Giroux and Kostas Myrsiades, *Beyond the Corporate University*. While the roots for the development of the contemporary university can be traced through many layers, we want to suggest that the flooding of university campuses with veterans whose funding was explicitly linked to vocational training laid the groundwork for the emergence of business and engineering schools and, indeed, regional comprehensive universities more broadly. The ideal of the liberal arts college, itself a historical construction that often elided other types of education and educational institutions, could not hold up against the sheer weight of the numbers of young men using veterans' benefits, and, perhaps more to the point, GI Bill funding had larger purposes in mind than simply a well-educated citizenry. It had in mind the creation of jobs and the creation of pathways to new jobs.[8]

The 1944 GI Bill explicitly authorized payment to types of institutions that might provide a clear pathway to future employment. Indeed, the words *training* and *vocational* appear with as much regularity as do terms like *education* or even *university*, and the types of schools that were codified as appropriate places of postservice learning illustrate the vocational focus of veteran education within the bill:

> As used in this part, the term educational or training institutions shall include all public or private elementary, secondary, and other schools furnishing education for adults, business schools and colleges, scientific and technical institutions, colleges, vocational schools, junior colleges, teachers colleges, normal schools, professional schools, universities, and other educational institutions, and shall also include business or other establishments providing apprentice or other training on the job, including those under the supervision of an approved college or university or any State department of education, or any State apprenticeship agency or State board of vocational education, or any State apprenticeship council of the Federal Apprentice Training Service. . . . (11a)

It is worth noting that education in this context could include work on a farm, what was called "institutional on-farm training," for which the student veteran received instruction and college credit as well. It also provided benefits for student veterans taking correspondence courses, either at home or abroad, as well as a "short, intensive postgraduate, or training course of less than thirty weeks" (3b {p. 8}). These types of educational pathways were codified as desirable by the 1944 GI Bill, and thousands of veterans took advantage of them. In doing so, they not only took advantage of a remarkable opportunity to pursue college educations, thereby forever changing the body politic of the United States, but they also carried with them an edict, sometimes explicit and sometimes implicit, which can most easily be summarized as "get to work." Education was the means to achieve that mission. What is different for today's veterans is the fact that the majority of jobs for skilled workers who lack a college education are in the service sector, rather than in the manufacturing or industrial sector. Consequently, opportunities to achieve social advancement without the benefit of a college degree are harder to come by, making educational benefits such as the GI Bill more appealing as a means to social mobility for some working-class families, a point overlooked by Giroux and other progressive critics.

WRITING, STASIS, AND ALIGNING VETERAN HIGHER EDUCATION

Within this "get to work" context, writing as a field, discipline, or mode of training barely registered. It remains that way today. Despite dramatic shifts in college curricula over the last seventy years, little has changed in the ways that veterans are encouraged to seek out postservice education. The reemergence of rhetoric and composition as a field in the 1970s and revisions of core curricula to emphasize first-year writing in the 1960s have had little impact on the notion of higher education as represented in the GI bills that followed the original, and the idea that writing could be central to the advancement of veterans within an information-rich culture is given little explicit consideration.

Such disciplinary invisibility is hardly noteworthy in itself, as policymakers seeking educational opportunities for veterans as a means for them to secure employment likely focus on skills that already have been taught to service members. To expect that any particular discipline, especially one within a humanistic tradition, would receive special notice within veteran education bills is asking too much of policymakers and probably would indicate explicit biases that most lawmakers would likely avoid anyway. Yet writing (and communication more broadly) has emerged as a central feature of undergraduate general education curricula and the contemporary workplace. While it was certainly embedded within curricula throughout the history of American higher education, since the middle of the twentieth century writing has secured a central place alongside mathematical instruction and scientific literacy. As writing has been codified as a central aspect of higher education, however, GI bill foci have remained decidedly unconcerned about writing instruction or even literacy more broadly.

To make such a claim is not to impugn the efforts or interests of those who have crafted the GI bills. Instead, it is to point out the historical impact of the original GI Bill and how its effect as a vocational bill, one whose purpose was explicitly to put veterans to work as quickly as possible, including on farms, continues to hold sway over veteran legislation (and some educators' preconceived notions of student veterans and their engagement in higher education). Put another way, the most recent GI Bill, if untethered from the original bill of the 1940s, when Agrarian America was giving way to Industrial America, may have looked very different if its primary influence had been today's cultural landscape. What would a GI bill look like if its primary educational agenda was to speak to today's transformation from the Industrial Age to the so-called "Information Age" or "Digital Age"? It would likely emphasize aspects of education that those earlier bills had no framework for considering, aspects that value new kinds of literacies and epistemologies.

Yet the residue of the initial educational motivations of the original bill remains. For example, in 2012, President Barack Obama, addressing students at a community college, argued explicitly that education was about creating jobs: "The goal isn't just making sure that somebody has got a certificate or a diploma. The goal is to make sure your degree helps you to get a promotion or a raise or a job. And that's especially important right now" (qtd. in Goldstein).

Education is described as a pathway to work here, a view that was written into the first GI Bill years before and that has expanded its reach ever since. Indeed, despite a veneer of a more technologically savvy or progressive GI Bill that advanced in Congress in 2017, the rationale for those revisions was grounded in the impulse toward vocation. At the front of the revisions for the Forever GI Bill were changes like extending the years allowable for veterans receiving benefits if they enrolled in certain STEM degrees or providing financial support for veterans seeking micro credentials in fields related to the technology sector. While these revisions aimed to make the GI Bill more progressive, they did so by reinforcing the predetermined goal of higher education as a vocational training ground. In each case, the impetus was to ensure that a student veteran's education was linked to distinct lines of work situated within a particular industry or employment sector. In other words, these revisions emphasized an education-as-job-training model with little regard for other aspects of postservice education.

Determining whether or not such foci are desirable is not the goal of this volume, but attending to this feature of the GI Bill is crucial if writing faculty or WPAs want to find ways to help student veterans progress in their college careers. Writing scholarship has already demonstrated the ways that many writing faculty face an identity crisis in a culture that may not readily recognize or value student writing or writing instruction. Kristen Kennedy, for example, points to the ways in which, "[a]s a field, we have done an excellent job . . . collecting the data that calcifies the portrait of rhetoric and composition as a field of sad women in basements, martyrs to the cause of literacy, and maligned and misunderstood intellectuals" (534). Laura Micciche addresses "the climate of disappointment" that characterizes writing program administration, which

> is shaped by a number of overlapping factors, including but not limited to the following: the widely perceived job market collapse in the humanities; national abuse of adjunct teachers whose primary duty is the instruction of required first-year writing courses; and the general devaluation of the humani-

ties as the academy develops into more and more of a corporate entity. (432)

And Marc Bousquet points to "current trends in the discourse, away from critical theory toward institutionally-focused pragmatism, toward acceptance of market logic, and toward increasing collaboration with a vocational and technical model of education" (13). When legislation codifies education in ways that may unwittingly erect barriers to students' understanding of the value of writing and advanced literacies, faculty engagement suffers. How does one teach writing to a student whose educational benefits urge them to privilege vocational degrees or degrees that are achievable in especially short time periods? How do writing instructors conceive of writing classes as relevant to students whose educational support may explicitly value other educational priorities? The answers are hardly simple, even if they are necessary to consider.

PRINCIPLES FOR FRAMING WRITING AS VOCATIONAL AFFORDANCE FOR VETERANS

Given the vocational framework of even the most recent GI Bill, those working in writing studies face both concrete and conceptual challenges in encouraging student veterans and their advocates to advance writing as requisite to veteran success in today's workplace and, indeed, contemporary American culture. It is striking that Americans today are more literate and more active writers and readers than any previous generation (see Yancey), and that despite much anxiety about education and literacy among young people, "millennials are," as Adrienne LaFrance's pointed headline proclaims, "out-reading older generations."

Considering the advanced literacy of today's world, then, two solutions for addressing the apparent absence of attention to writing as requisite for veteran success can be implemented by faculty regardless of legislative agendas, even if those solutions also present philosophical and practical challenges. The first is conceiving of the writing classroom as a place to practice transfer of knowledge and skills. The second is foregrounding the idea that writing, and literacy more broadly, is a tool of social mobility. Both of these ideas are already embedded in many curricula, yet both carry with them cultural references to the role of education that some educators may find limiting or reductive. Giroux (2008), for example, links the rise of "militarization" to a parallel rise in "neoliberalism" and the "corporatization" of higher education.[9]

Some of those limitations are discussed below, but at the heart of both of these solutions is that the writing classroom must, as a rhetorical space, consider its audience, and if student veterans are among its audience members, speaking a language and providing an education that is connected to the veterans' experience not only of the military, but of the GI Bill itself, will help student veterans connect their lives to the goals of college writing instruction. Put another way: because the language of the GI Bill shapes the educational experience of veterans using it, writing faculty would be wise to connect to that language in advancing their classroom practices. As Michele Eodice, Anne Ellen Geller, and Neal Lerner discovered, "when prior knowledge is conceptualized in narrow ways," writing instruction might "disrupt any potential connections to students' passions, experiences, and identities, which [their] study shows are key to meaningful writing experiences" (96–97). Studies of transfer provide possibilities here.

Principle 1: Conceive of the Writing Classroom as a Place to Practice Transfer of Knowledge and Skills

Jenn Fishman and Mary Jo Reiff provide an example of how to highlight transfer when they describe a complete overhaul of their composition program to emphasize transfer, and Julie Dyke Ford discusses a restructuring of a mechanical engineering curriculum component to focus on transferable metacognitive processes. Elizabeth Wardle has argued convincingly that first-year writing (FYW), though a starting place for writing transfer, is hardly alone sufficient for advancing core writing concepts and making them transferable across institutional, let alone workplace, contexts. Much of the research is qualitative and ethnographic, yet it all points to the notion that a transfer-aware or transfer-oriented classroom provides fertile ground for knowledge "uptake."

One of the best ways to achieve that goal is to orient writing classrooms explicitly toward practicing transfer of knowledge and skills. A healthy body of recent research testifies to the value of deliberate focus on transfer in classes. For example, Doug Brent has discussed various waves of transfer research, noting that transfer as a concept for classrooms emerged from a "closing the gap" model that sought to help students connect classroom work to vocational goals. For student veterans this model may be especially helpful, as research on veteran transitions shows time and again that among the greatest obstacles to veteran success in college is a "disconnect" between military and civilian educational experiences (see Chapter 3). Writing instructors sensitive to this fact can help bridge the gap by helping students recognize and articulate how military experiences can be transferred as tools for learning in civilian educational settings. In fact, research shows that "in an expansive environment, one in which students are positioned as authors whose knowledge from prior settings is considered welcome, students are more likely to transfer-in knowledge during learning in ways that can enhance later transfer out" (Engle et al., qtd. in Eodice, Geller, and Lerner 98). Doing so requires faculty to understand the types of education service members receive while in the military, even as it requires students to describe and reflect on those experiences as formative to their current educational agendas and future career goals.

In fact, as we discuss in more detail in both Chapter 1 and Chapter 3, and as we hope the interstitial chapters illustrate, many veterans have already engaged in a wide range of writing practices within military environments. Faculty awareness of the types of writing veterans may have done within the military only helps in the process of transfer. The more knowledgeable a faculty member can be about types of writing within military contexts, the more they can promote expansive learning and help students transfer the core skills within those contexts to the new civilian one. Some of the samples of writing in this volume's writing/practices interchapters were done by service members or by writers in a military context. The goal of these samples is, on the one hand, to demonstrate the diversity of writing experiences within the military by providing a glimpse into the range of writing done across different branches and ranks, while, on the other hand, illustrating some of the core tenets of writing that veterans may carry with them into the writing classroom. Many of those tenets—perspicuity, clarity, specificity, inclusiveness—are likely to resonate with many writing instructors today. When they do, writing faculty may be able to see how, and why, attending to military writing (e.g., by using expansive framing to "[take] into account students' personal connection to their topics and their interests in their writing as relevant to their futures" [Eodice, Geller, and Lerner 97]) might help them articulate why writing instruction can be a central aspect of student veterans' educational *and* vocational aspirations.

Principle 2: Foreground the Idea That Writing Is a Tool of Social Mobility

The range of writing experiences with specific career outcomes within the military itself suggests that writing functions as a tool for social mobility, a fact that might help faculty reorient the goals of their own core curriculum. Such a move, of course, might be regarded as contrary to the goals of a traditional liberal arts curriculum, and indeed, it may be seen as pandering to the ever-encroaching power of the "corporate" university. Yet a college degree remains to this day the surest route to socioeconomic advancement (see *Fact Sheet*), and writing remains one of the most sought-after skills in today's marketplace (see *Fulfilling*). Such facts need not undo a classical approach to education that values the ideals of an educated citizenry, even if they do present challenges for WPAs and writing instructors, in particular, who are, as more than one commentator has pointed out (C. Nelson; Micciche; Malenczyk et al.), under pressure to demonstrate their worth in systems that rely on standardized outcomes and quantitative measures that purport to prepare students for "real life."

Suggesting that writing helps students in their vocational aspirations is a short step from arguing that writing is central to their college education, but the growing evidence that communication skills are central to social advancement illustrates how veterans and the military community more broadly might rethink what it means to seek further instruction in writing. Ample evidence testifies to the fact that writing is highly valued as a pathway toward career advancement. For example, in an article posted to the *NCO [noncommissioned officer] Journal*, a publication of the Army University Press, Crystal Bradshaw contends, "Writing is now, more than ever, a core component in NCOs' weekly responsibilities. The ability to effectively articulate your thoughts and verbal words into writing can ensure that you are able to establish your professionalism and may help you advance through the ranks." In a 2017 article for *Military Review*, Army Major Hassan Kamara argues, "An increased emphasis on writing can help the Army effectively utilize the soldier expertise it is cultivating through sustained investments in education" and thereby "enhance soldier competence, innovation, and critical thinking" (115). To substantiate his claims that writing "promotes institutional learning, adaptation, and innovation," Kamara provides several examples such as, "during the Iraq and Afghanistan campaigns, units were able to share operational lessons by providing written feedback from their combat tours to centralized forums such as the Center for Army Lessons Learned, and in many cases directly to the units replacing them" (117). Ultimately, as Mark Blaauw-Hara points out, "All formal military writing—regardless of whether it is a log entry produced by a private, a counseling report produced by a sergeant, or a memorandum produced by an officer—is an important contribution to the military enterprise" ("Learning").

If this is true within the military, it is no less true in the civilian sector. Annual surveys of skills most demanded by employers regularly place writing and communication skills at the top of the list, so embracing the idea that education in writing leads to better socioeconomic conditions does not require one to embrace the "corporatization" of the university, whatever that may be. It requires only a commitment to the idea that education matters, not just in the sense of being a better person or living the proverbial examined life, but in the sense of lived experiences of groups of people who, without more advanced literacy, would continue to struggle in a culture that requires extensive literacies in order to thrive. Military culture, in particular, places a high premium on training in skills that not only advance potential employment after a military career, but simultaneously grounds those skills in broader ethical considerations. The move toward skills training, in other words, does not represent within military culture the abdication of ethical or moral considerations; indeed, many aspects of military training require the joining of both, so that the practical is yoked to ideals such as service, sacrifice, and honor. Higher education might find within that culture a similar vision, where consideration of employment prospects is not a de facto skirting of the goals of advanced education, but instead represents conjoined processes for social mobility and security. Indeed, the very term *work ethic* implies within its structure a latent relationship between work and moral obligations to one's communities and to oneself.

Veterans, as they make the transition into civilian life, therefore need the same tools for social advancement that traditional students do. Examining how veterans have already cultivated some of those skills, including writing, as part of their military careers, only positions them to take greater advantage of what our writing classrooms offer (see Blaauw-Hara). Helping them place their already rich writing experiences within a new context helps them to anticipate how writing might fit into future contexts, ones that align with their aspirations outside of the university. By doing so, we as writing instructors can foster a sense of inclusion for a group that often feels isolated.

Chapter 2 Implementation Questions

- Does your curriculum actively promote considerations of writing transfer?
- Does your campus provide resources to help veterans connect their work experiences in the military to their work as students?
- Does your campus actively recruit veterans using GI Bill benefits? Is your campus a Yellow Ribbon campus?

- Which writing outcomes within your curriculum share similarities to outcomes for writing within the military?
- Which writing outcomes within your curriculum aim to help students connect their classroom writing to writing for their professions or for their vocational goals?

Writing/Practices 1

Student Voices/Writing Genres

UNDERSTANDING THE ASSETS VETERANS POSSESS
AND TRANSFER TO THE WRITING CLASSROOM

IN THIS SECTION, WE PRESENT EXAMPLES of student veteran writing to illustrate how these students negotiate rhetorical genres. The first is a speech by a female service member delivered at a university event. She reflects on her time in service in order to provide a sense of her development as both a military service member and a student considering new career options. The second is a piece of classroom writing done by a former Marine that responds to texts about war. He connects the experiences he read about in class to his own experiences in combat. The final is a set of emails by an Army officer who would later go on to get an advanced degree in education. We include these emails to signal how personal writing to specific audiences is a common part of many service members' experiences.

Example 1
Sherry Shi's Veterans Day Speech
Stony Brook University has an annual Veterans Day event that includes a guest speaker as well as a short speech by the leadership of the Veterans Student Organization. The process for the composition of the speech is marked by peer review and revision. Sherry Shi, who would intern at the White House and now works for Facebook, was an officer in the student veteran group on campus and drafted the speech on her own. She then sent a copy to the head of veterans affairs on campus, who made suggestions. She subsequently made revisions and gave practice readings to the veterans affairs committee, a group of about ten people, including university staff, faculty, and students, who provided feedback

*on both the written document and Sherry's oral presentation. After final
revisions, Sherry practiced the speech a couple of days prior to the Veterans Day ceremony on site at the ceremony location. The process was
highly collaborative and notable for its inclusion of revision suggestions
from a wide variety of stakeholders and audience members. Within the
speech below, we include comments to illustrate how Sherry negotiates
the genre of an epideictic speech even as she connects a narrative of her
time in service to her career aspirations.*

Good afternoon, everyone, my name is Sherry Shi and I'm a student veteran here at Stony Brook. I joined the United States Army
in 2008, when I was seventeen, straight out of high school. When
people find out I'm a veteran, the first question I usually get is,
"How many people have you killed?" The second question I get is,
"Why did you decide to join the military?" *[These questions are a
direct attempt to connect to veterans in the audience. They are questions
that many veterans report fielding from civilians.]* Well, I don't exactly
have a generic answer to this question. I didn't need the college
money, it wasn't my lifelong dream to become a soldier, and it defi-
nitely isn't a family tradition. So why did I join? The best answer
I can really give is that I wasn't ready to graduate high school and
go straight into college. I wasn't sure what my passions were, and
having skipped a grade, I had a year less than my friends to figure
that out. I don't think anyone should have to waste money getting a
degree in a field of study that they don't like, just because it's what's
expected of you in today's society. *[Notice here the appeal to the idea
of self-discovery that challenges the idea that college is the place of self-
discovery. Here, the military takes on the role, with college taking on the
role of career preparation.]*
    Believe it or not, it was actually my dad who suggested that I
join the military. At first I was pretty skeptical. But after I talked
to a recruiter, my viewpoint was completely changed. About two
months later, on my seventeenth birthday, I signed a contract to
enlist in the U.S. Army. And I must say it was the best decision I
have made yet.
    In the four years that I served, I have traveled the world, made life
friends from around the globe, and served my country. Of course,

it wasn't all fun and games. There's basic training, there's waking up at 5:00 a.m. every morning to go get yelled at, do pushups, or run several miles, and there's constantly being criticized for not living up to every little military standard. But you kinda get used to the lifestyle after a while, and it kinda starts to grow on you.

My official military occupation specialty was Intelligence Analyst. I did my basic training in Fort Leonard Wood, Missouri, and my job training in Fort Huachuca, Arizona. After that, I was stationed in Germany for a year, I did a year's deployment in Baghdad, Iraq, and then I was back to Germany for the remainder of my service. In Iraq, I was actually assigned to many duties that did not pertain to my occupation specialty. *[Here is a crucial point. Shi connects her specific expertise to other jobs she was required to do. This is the foundation of transfer thinking that we explore in this volume.]* I primarily worked with the systems maintainers and the IT helpdesk technicians. Sometimes I would just troubleshoot computer and networking issues in our division headquarters for the soldiers and higher-ranking officers who worked there. Other times I'd have to travel to different bases throughout Iraq to help set up networks for other units, including for the Iraqi Army.

To sum it up, in the year I was in Iraq, there were great times but there were also miserable and dangerous times. But in the end I am so happy that I was able to serve my country. I was honorably discharged in February 2012 as a sergeant. Through the Army I not only gained new friendships and incredible experiences, but I also discovered so many things about myself. One of the things I realized is that I really do love working with computers, as well as with other people.

This is currently my second year at Stony Brook, and I am majoring in computer science. I'm the vice president of our Veterans Student Organization and also the webmaster for the Women in Computer Science club. I'm hoping to eventually continue working for the government, but as a civilian. Maybe get a master's in international relations. I did not end up choosing the military as a career, but it has molded my path for the rest of my life, and I hope that my story will be able to help a few others find theirs as well.

Thank you!

Example 2
August Oetting Research Paper

The student writing below, by August Oetting, a Marine Corps OEF veteran and Stony Brook University graduate, offers an analysis of the representation of trauma in three Iraq War memoirs. That analysis is couched within his experiences as a combat veteran. While not explicitly labeling his own experience as traumatic, August nonetheless describes surviving an IED explosion as an ordering moment in his own life, a rhetorical move that then functions as a framing device by which he enters into a process of analysis. That analysis focuses on the representation of trauma, and he ends his discussion by returning to the impact of not only the books, but, more poignantly, also the IED explosion on his daily life.

Trauma in August's essay is something experienced by others, represented in the memoirs he read for class but not fully embodied by his own experience. Despite identifying signs of trauma in his own daily life in the conclusion of the essay, August's work illustrates the ambivalence some student veterans feel in grouping their experience with the "more traumatic" experiences of their peers. August's work here shows he can identify with the trauma of Shannon Meehan and David Bellavia, and he connects those with the trauma of an Iraqi expatriate, Wafaa Bilal, but at the same time the analysis insists on a boundary around trauma delineated by degree—a "not as bad as the other guy" mentality that emerges frequently with student veterans and in a variety of ways. As we've discussed in other places throughout this book, especially with regard to seeking support in their writing process, student veterans may choose not to seek writing center appointments or appointments with faculty if they believe others may need help more. Similarly, they may minimize their own needs in the face of the needs of a class as a whole, a team-first mentality. August's conclusion implies some of this, even as it uses concrete, palpable language to identify the results of trauma in his own life.

August's essay illustrates his attempts to negotiate the demands of analysis within the context of both personal narrative and research. The framing of the essay by narrative provides readers with a clear sense of the relevance of the readings to his own life, even as the subsequent analysis negotiates the more traditional demands of an academic research essay. It integrates source work and builds a claim by moving from one text to another. This deployment of analytic support for an assertion resembles the basic outline of a military brief, even as the narrative around that support does not. The joining of the narrative with the analytic is an attempt to expand his understanding of genre to include the personal.

August was not active in the veterans' student group on the Stony Brook campus, but he displayed his military identity proudly. He readily disclosed his veteran status early in the class and actively sought opportunities to share his experiences with other students in class. While in conversation he noted differences between his life's priorities and the focus of many of his class peers, he embraced the diversity of experience and recognized that his goals, formed through his experiences, would necessarily be different from those of others. He met with his professor frequently, and he earnestly sought to improve his writing, realizing that it was a tangible skill that could advance his career. His professor informs all classes that writings done for his assignments are effectively "public" documents that will be peer-revised and that he will share with university resource professionals any information he thinks is useful in providing support for students. His professor already had a standing relationship with the veterans' affairs director, so he discussed August's work in broad terms with him and encouraged August to make contact with that office to see whether that community would be helpful to him. August excelled in school and now works as a nurse in California.

War: No Place to Hide
August Oetting, Stony Brook University

Author's Note:
> "It has been said, 'time heals all wounds.' I do not agree. The wounds remain. In time, the mind, protecting its sanity, covers them with scar tissue and the pain lessens. But it is never gone."
> —Rose Kennedy

"I won't let you have him. I want him back. And I don't care if you have to rot in hell but you will lose. I hope you're ready. PTSD, I hate you . . . "

—Heather Goble

I have been down the roads of Bellavia and Meehan, with the exception of being on the brink of losing my life. *[In the opening sentence, Oetting connects his experience to the class texts but is careful to draw a distinction about trauma.]* During my first deployment to Afghanistan, I witnessed the death of an insurgent and I had my vehicle be blown up by an Improvised Explosive Device. The explosion left everyone in the truck with mostly minor wounds, scrapes, cuts, and bruises. All these things heal and go away, maybe leaving a small scar; but the experiences will forever be seared into my brain. My everyday life has been altered in a major way, compared to what it was like before the Marine Corps. I had never worried about an intruder in my home, or even how to handle that situation. I had never worried about a stranger wandering into a classroom with a weapon, with the intent to harm people. I had never worried about being attacked while taking trash to the road at night. Now my days are constantly filled with thoughts of the worst-case scenario, and whether I'm prepared to handle what I, logically, most likely won't face. Road trips are filled with the random anticipation of the highly unlikely chance my car runs over a bomb or takes bullets from an invisible enemy. This doesn't make life easy by any means and my ability to keep these impulses at bay around my family only makes me wonder how much support I can provide those in my life.

The invisible wounds have damaged the lives of billions and billions of people throughout history and only now, in modern days, do we begin to understand them. By understanding these wounds, we can find new ways to assist in prevention of them and the consequences. But, until that day, civilians and service members will forever be mentally scarred from the events of the world around them that they were thrown into with or without their consent. Meehan in *Beyond Duty,* Bellavia in *House to House,* and Bilal in *Shoot an*

Iraqi have recovered from physical wounds just to have their lives impacted by mental injuries.

Shannon Meehan's experiences that he faced during his time in Iraq have propelled him into a life of daily troubles and uncertainties. Meehan had encountered multiple events that changed his life. The last event we are audience for is when Shannon heads back to the trucks after a long day clearing a village. He decides to take an alternate route back. He led his troops down a canal, that he presumed the enemy used to travel. In a split second Meehan found himself thrown into the air. He sustained major injuries (168). These wounds he sustained from the IED he stepped on eventually all healed. He made enough of a physical recovery that he was allowed to return to his men. Before he was cleared to go back to the battlefield, he was to undergo a psychological evaluation. The day prior to his return, he was asked by a doctor a series of questions. The doctor told Meehan, "You just used the word 'worthless' more times than I can count." He continued and told Shannon, "I think you're depressed . . . " (175) Although Meehan was allowed to return to his men, the doctor and himself both knew he was not okay. Yes, physically he was mostly healed, but mentally he was beginning to suffer from events that are only seen in a war zone.

Shannon's depression wasn't solely stemming from the fact that he had seen death during war or that he himself had almost been killed, but it resonates also from an air strike he called in on a house. Meehan had suspected that the house was rigged to explode when American troops entered. Having learned from a similar event a few months prior, Meehan made the decision to blow the house up. An unforeseen result of his actions was the death of a family. Eight civilians (140–42). This catastrophic event broke Shannon. The image of the family was instantly burned into his mind. "I can't shake it, and no matter how hard I try, I can't project it outward. I can't forget it and I can't make others see it. It just simply lingers there, suspended and dark in the shadows of my mind" (143). These few lines are important to the reader because of both the imagery of lingering effect, and also the problem of discussing events that impact one's life drastically. The words "shadows" and "dark" give you the visual ugliness of depression, and "suspended" and "lingers" give you the feeling of the dead weight carried with not being able to rid yourself of the evil events of war. Meehan also hints at the issues of not being able to discuss and open up to people about what has happened to yourself. The feeling that nobody would understand, no matter how much detail you describe to someone.

After his return home, Shannon continued to devalue his accomplishments. On New Year's Eve, when AJ and the rest of his family threw a celebration for him, when he started thinking about his service to America, he stated, "I realized that my service, which I once had shown with pride, had become a mark of failure. I turned further inward and further away from any hope that I could ever feel okay" (183). Eight years removed from his deployment in Iraq, Shannon has overcome the sense of failure, and through discussing the events and with the support of family and friends, he managed to write his book and find pride and lessons in everything he has faced (Shannon Meehan, Interview, 5/5/2016). On page 188, Meehan talks more about how it's been a year since he called in the missile strike, and how he still has to stop, pause, and hold back a little when it comes to talking about it. Shannon's wife, AJ, tolerates the struggles Shannon has talking about the events. She is understanding to the fact that he may not always be mentally present.

> *"I heard sometimes you could be two places at once—physically in one place but mentally elsewhere."*
> —Heather Goble

[Notice here the use of external authority to validate a central point. Appeals to authority are central to many types of military writing, which values hierarchies as demonstrations of knowledge, skills, and power.]

"I should be happy, right? Right? *What is wrong with me."* (311) Bellavia begins to describe Christmas Day with Deanna and his two little boys. He says how the boys ripping open gifts, the fire going, and the "Lake Erie-style blizzard" makes for the perfect day. However, it isn't the perfect day. Deanna and Bellavia both know this isn't where he is mentally. His wife and himself both know he isn't ready to put family first. His head is stuck in Iraq. The thoughts of something missing flood his mind. "You bet there's something missing. Sean Sims. Edward Iwan, Sergeant-Major. Rosales and Sizemore. They're all missing" (312). After a little longer of being tormented by his past experiences, he snaps back to Christmas Day. They get ready to take a picture, and as his sons begin to pose, Bellavia is teleported back to his days in Iraq. He describes the killing of what he believed to be two brothers. The two were in a similar pose as his sons. He continues to talk about how he could never imagine his kids going through war (318).

Bellavia tells his audience that he will never be the same person that he was before the day of his house fight. "My innocence is gone" (318). The house fight he is referring to is the brutal and horrific hand-to-hand fight against the enemy. Ultimately, he had to kill an insurgent with his bare hands, while he himself was on the edge of dying. It was bloody and savage fight (249—89). This fight left Bellavia severely wounded, but these wounds healed. The ones that didn't heal are the ones that will never be overcome. Bellavia has to live with his actions in Iraq and they have affected, and will continue to affect, his everyday life. He may forever be pulled from the current family party, and sent back to where his sane mentality will forever remain, Fallujah.

Not everyone who is impacted by war has an event that takes place that maims their body. *[The section here on a book written by an Iraqi national is the shortest. Notice the less-developed connection between the author's experiences and Oetting's even as Oetting uses it as a springboard to introduce his own experience in his conclusion].* Mr. Bilal, in *Shoot an Iraqi,* doesn't necessarily fall victim to physicals wounds of war. However, he is no stranger to the emotions and events that take place as a civilian dealing with a war in your country's backyard. Wafaa grew up in Iraq under Saddam Hussein's rule. His early life was plastered with senseless deaths of both Americans and Iraqi civilians. Wafaa lost both his father and brother, and his mother and sister remained in Iraq. Wafaa feels profound guilt in what has happened in his past and leaving his family behind. He comes up with the idea of his experiment "Domestic Tension." The principle of the experiment is to show the underlying tensions that exist in America. Wafaa puts himself into a box with a paintball gun that people can sign into online and shoot. Wafaa's month-long experiment put him under extreme stress and public ridicule of people saying derogatory statements against him. Wafaa's emotional past and experiences are forever ingrained in his mind. These events affected and will continue to affect how he lives he life.

Anxiety. Paranoia. Sleep deprivation. Depression. Frustration. Angry issues. Forgetfulness. *[A notable shift here from analytic writing to one of personal expression. The shift in sentence structure reflects a shift from both summary and analysis (key features of, for example, both military briefs and analytic essays in college) to personal expressions of life experiences.]* These are aspect of my life now. These are aspects of a lot of service members' and civilians' lives as well. They have changed us, both equally good and bad. These invisible wounds lead to Post-Traumatic Stress Disorder (PTSD), a mental health problem that effects the mental states of individuals who have been involved in traumatic events (http://www.ptsd.va.gov/). PTSD has recently been in the spotlight of society due to the rise in veteran suicides. On average, twenty-two veterans take their lives every day. The only way to protect these war heroes is to recognize the signs early and support the veterans the best we can. This means encouraging veterans to be open about the events of their lives and that we be understanding in what they have to say. Ignorance is no excuse for not saving a suffering veteran's or civilian's life.

> *"I'd heard you'd been violent before, or in instances like ours, cowardly, disguising yourself as miracle pills that would end the suffering you've caused."*

—Heather Goble

WORKS CITED

Bilal, Wafaa, and Kari Lydersen. *Shoot an Iraqi: Art, Life and Resistance under the Gun.* City Lights Publishers, 2008.

Bellavia, David, and John Bruning. *House to House: A Soldier's Memoir.* Free Press, 2007.

Heather Goble, "Dear PTSD: Letter from a Military Wife to the Condition Destroying Her Family." *Business Insider,* 5 July 2012, www.businessinsider.com/dear-ptsd-letter-from-a-military-wife-2012-7.

Meehan, Shannon P., with Roger Thompson. *Beyond Duty: Life on the Frontline in Iraq,* Polity Press, 2009.

Example 3
Shannon Meehan's Email Correspondence
The early parts of OEF and OIF occurred just as email became the primary mode of communication for American culture. Email provided near-instantaneous contact with home and led to the military's having to rethink its policies around service members' communications with family and friends. We include here a small sampling of emails from Shannon Meehan, whose memoir Roger Thompson cowrote. We would draw attention to the ways that the emails assumed swift responses and the way that they drew attention to the broader impact of media on communication.

Assignments for composing sample emails or letters are not uncommon in today's classrooms, and those lessons often emphasize audience considerations. Here, Meehan's personal emails reveal a very clear sense of audiences, and indeed, also illustrate the diversity of the audiences who may have access to them. Helping student veterans recall their own writing experiences with artifacts like emails while in service by drawing attention to audience consideration and even format of the genre can help students transfer their knowledge of audience to other genres of writing.

16 March 2006

Just wishing everyone a Happy St. Patrick's Day!!

PS. If you pick up a copy of today's (Fri) Daily Times, *[In the emails that follow, notice how Meehan connects his audience to other types of writing about his own deployment]* you will see this monkey pic made it all the way to the papers! Also, there will be an article on the 4 yr anniversary of the war in Sunday's edition of the daily times, so be sure to read it if you can.

Have a great, fun & safe weekend!!!

Shannon

20 March 2006

Hey Guys,

In case you missed it, The Daily Times wrote a very interesting piece on the 4 year mark on the war. It is a provocative article including opinions from several different sources with several different outlooks on the war.

I was interviewed for the article, and even little AJ snuck in the paper with a great picture of the two of us together, as so did . . . the famous monkey pic. [*Meehan here refers to a set of photographs with which he knows his audience is familiar.*] Well I hope all is well with everyone, and I will be back again in October, for good . . . as long as we don't get extended. I hope to see you all at that time. Enjoy . . .

19 November 2006

Hey All,

Yes it's me again already. I just wanted to let you guys know that my platoon made the news today, due to the 6 hour fire-fight (battle) yesterday (Nov 18th). I saw the story on yahoo.com, and other sites, and there was a picture of one of my sergeants with a colonel. The battle was in down-town Bacuba, and it consisted of my 15 Soldiers and I, an army Colonel, and Iraqi Army soldiers (about 20) that we are in charge of training. We engaged enemy insurgents within the city, drove them back to the palm groves on the city's edge and defeated them with only one casualty (an I.A. soldier).

I am recommending many of my soldiers for awards from the battle as they again performed well.

Could someone - AJ - let my family (mom/dad) know too & maybe print the story out for them to read.

I hope all is well with everybody at home, and I look forward to all of your next emails letting me know whats up & how you are doing.

Stay safe & have fun. And I love you AJ ;)

-Shannon

UNDERSTANDING THE WRITING STANDARDS AND GENRES VETERANS MIGHT BRING TO THE WRITING CLASSROOM

In this section, we provide examples of military writing guidance and genres to draw attention to some of the shared rhetorical strategies and conventions. The first piece is an excerpt from an Air Force writing handbook (though we want to note that each branch of the military has its own equivalent style guide). We follow this excerpt with a sample template for an Army After-Action Review (AAR), a common genre produced in the service. The final piece is an essay published in the Air Force periodical *Combat Crew*.

Writing Standards: *The Tongue and Quill*, United States Air Force

The Air Force has used a style book, The Tongue and Quill, *for decades, and it has gone through several revisions over the span of its lifetime. Below, we quote from two iterations of the book in order to demonstrate the way that rhetorical instruction has been a part of writing life within the Air Force and the way that feedback from peers and attention to the "target audience" has been integrated into the system to the degree that conceptual growth of ideas derives from feedback or even rejection.*

We would draw attention to certain aspects of the text. First, notice the emphasis on the process of communication. Communication here is figured as dynamic and fluid. The second example illustrates this in a way that is likely familiar to most composition teachers. It includes a discussion of rhetorical principles that are often the foundation of today's writing classrooms. Our point is that the distance between military modes of written communication and genres of college writing may not be as great as many might expect. Faculty may be able to ease student veteran transition by appealing to some of the same language with which some of them have been educated in the military. The focus on audience and intent may be especially productive for faculty to consider.

From a 1997 version of the text, we find especially direct statements on the power of feedback:

> Perhaps you got the impression that successful communications [consist] of making sure you remove the barriers and clean up your logic. Right? Nope. Expect legitimate disagreements or unalterably opposed viewpoints, even when the communication is thoroughly effective in design and execution. Does this mean your communication is doomed to fail because it's planted counter to current philosophy or a particular viewpoint? Not necessarily. Years ago Tamotsu Shibutani wrote *Improvised News . . . A Sociological Study of Rumor.* He vividly described the importance of the phenomenon of time dimension in human communications. Ideas, once heard, cannot be erased and perceptions are constantly changing. Don't take the initial rejection of your idea as a failure to communicate. You may be surprised to find the idea has sprouted after weeks, months or even years have passed! You planted a "seed" with your communication, and that seed might germinate and be fertilized by other communications heard or seen by the target audience. *[Note here the use of the term* target audience, *a term also used by college writing instructors.]* Eventually, that seed (perhaps a new idea you were trying to sell) is accepted by the target audience (your boss, perhaps?). So fear not—go forth and plant seeds. (5)

The colloquial tone of the 1997 version is replaced in the 2015 version, but the focus on explicitly rhetorical principles (e.g., the rhetorical triangle) that will be quite familiar to today's writing studies faculty are highlighted, coming earlier in the book and also more explicitly stated in it:

> Communication is defined as the process of sharing ideas, information and messages with others. In the Air Force, most communication involves speaking and writing, but this defi-

nition also includes nonverbal communication, such as body language, graphics, electronic messages, etc.

Any communication can be broken into three parts: the *sender*, the *message* and the *audience*. *[Notice here a version of Bitzer's rhetorical situation.]* For communication to be successful, the audience must not only get the message, but must interpret the message in the way the sender intended. *[Notice here the centrality of audience and how intent must be framed in ways that audiences can receive.]*

Since communication requires effort, it should always have a purpose. *[Like the familiar emphasis on audience, the military guidelines also highlight purpose in relation to audience. Indeed, some student veterans may be more familiar with these terms from the rhetorical situation than are some students entering straight out of American high schools.]* If the purpose isn't clear to the audience, you have a problem! Most Air Force communication is intended to direct, inform (or educate), persuade or inspire. Often the sender has some combination of these motives in mind.

Chapter 3 describes the process of determining your purpose and audience in detail, but here are a few examples of Air Force communication targeted toward a specific objective:

1. The headquarters staff (the sender); writes a new policy on trip report procedures (the message); and sends a copy to all subordinate units (the audience).
   Purpose of this communication: to direct.
2. An aircraft technician (the sender); reports the results of an aircraft engine inspection (the message); to his supervisor (the audience).
   Purpose of this communication: to inform.
3. A branch chief (the sender); requests additional funding for new office furniture (the message); in a meeting with the division chief (the audience).
   Purpose of this communication: to persuade.

Most communication outside the Air Force falls in these categories as well. (4)

Military Writing Genre: After-Action Review

The following excerpt from a sample of an After-Action Review (or in this case Report) (AAR) comes from guidance from the website for the Under Secretary of Defense for Acquisition, Technology, and Logistics (now Acquisition and Sustainment). It is intended to provide a model for an AAR within that unit and demonstrates both the standard features of the genre as well as, in this case, a discussion of the way that language is itself a consideration in the issue being raised by the report. The AAR is a widely used genre within the military, and it has been historically positioned as a document that prompts thoughtful and engaged review of an activity or event. As one leadership manual for the Army states: "Key is the spirit in which AARs are given. The environment and climate surrounding an AAR must be one in which the soldiers and leaders openly and honestly discuss what actually transpired in sufficient detail and clarity that not only will everyone understand what did and did not occur and why, but most importantly will have a strong desire to seek the opportunity to practice the task again" ("Leader's Guide"). The AAR, in other words, provides a written contingency that lends to preparedness by mitigating other standing military hierarchies in order to ensure fruitful discussion.

AFTER ACTION REPORT SAMPLE

DEPARTMENT OF THE XXXXX
MILITARY ORGANIZATION
BASE NAME AIR FORCE BASE, STATE, Country, etc. . . .

MEMORANDUM FOR:
FROM:
SUBJECT: After Action Report,

1. This after action report is prepared IAW XXXX *[The outline format of an AAR allows for clarity in organization. Such organizational standardization provides a heuristic for writers, allowing them to gen-*

erate ideas in a specific order to reach a desired outcome. Faculty may find such organizational structures limiting, but consideration of their inventional aspects allows for new approaches to writing assignments whose focus is on arrangement or organization.]

2. The following is information regarding the contingency itself:
   Deployed Location:
   Deployed CCOs:
   Duration of Site Survey:
   Duration of Deployment:
   Contingency Purpose: In support of _____.

3. *Potential Sources of Supply:* See attached list of vendors, items supplied, phone numbers and POCs. Sources were plentiful for the majority of items. Most businesses belonged to a group, or conglomerate, so if one business did not have what you were looking for they could usually refer you to someone who could provide for your needs.

   a. *Host Nation Support*: The _____ provided some furniture, aircraft maintenance space and jersey barbers. An acquisition agreement with the _____ for ground fuel was written by CENTAF.

   b. *U.S. EMBASSY:* We did not use the embassy for sourcing. They did consent to handling the payment of the phone bill for all the phones at the installation since an invoice could not be obtained prior to redeployment. Finance completed a military pay request (MIPR) which transferred funds to the U.S. Embassy enabling them to make payment.

   c. *Servicing U.S. Military Installations:* The _____ helped with some small purchases. They sourced and procured some desert nametapes and Gatorade, which was unavailable in _____.

   d. *Local Transportation, Billeting, and Communication Resource Availability:* BPAs were established with all the local car rental agencies in order to meet all the transportation requirements. [*Military writing often uses passive voice, but veteran students may not be familiar with that term or understand the logic behind using passive constructions.*] A shortage of rental vehicles exists in _____.

Utility vehicles are scarce as well as passenger vans. The U.S. Army is currently in _____, establishing a permanent post and had most of the utility vehicles rented. We discussed the possibility of accidents and payment before renting the cars and both parties understood the correct procedure. However, we did experience difficulties with our customers following the correct procedures. All personnel were restricted to the installation, so all the accidents occurred on the camp. All accidents in _____require a _____ civilian police accident report. In _____, without an accident report the company's insurance will *not cover* the costs of the damages. There were some instances where accidents occurred and the _____ Police were never called out to the site to complete an accident report. Days went by before the police were actually called, so the police report did not state who was at fault for the accident. The company's insurance would not cover the damages due to the negligence of the government for not following the proper procedures. A settlement for the damages was reached, but could have been avoided had the customers followed the proper procedures as briefed. Ensure all companies understand that all insurance and damage risks are at the expense of the contractor and that all your vehicles have full coverage insurance. In addition, ensure all personnel are briefed on the proper procedures for accidents and damages. Recommend reserving as many utility vehicles as far in advance as possible. Cars are not meant to be driven on the rough terrain that exists on the installation. A few cars were damaged from driving on the terrain. The Government had to pay for these damages which could have been avoided had more utility vehicles been provided by the Air Force since the supply of local utility vehicles is so low.

BPAs were established with four of the local hotels for billeting. Only the Sheraton _____ BPA was utilized since everyone was restricted to the camp. The only personnel that resided downtown in the hotel were Finance and Contracting. It was vital to the success of the mission that Contracting and the paying agent remain downtown in order to provide a professional meeting place as well as expedient delivery of supplies. Due to contracting and finance working together in the hotel, vendors were able to receive payment, drop off supplies, discuss important concerns in person with no hassles of waiting in long lines at the gate or having to go through the tedious process of obtaining a pass. The end result was customer satisfaction and mission success.

Cellular telephones were rented from two different contractors in order to meet our requirements. These were invaluable communication tools throughout the deployment. These were essential for contracting officers. It allowed us to stay in constant communication with each other and with personnel at the site. Our Logistic Group commander, who approved all purchases for the deployment, could contact his contracting officers at any time with requests or questions. Business over the phone could be conducted at any place and saved us a tremendous amount of time. COMM took approximately two weeks in setting up the telephone network and took it down approximately one week prior to redeployment. The cellular phones allowed us to stay in touch with all of our major customers when questions or concerns arose. Recommend Services and CE have cellular phones throughout the entire deployment. Open communication is vital to the success of the deployment. A daily meeting should be held with all your major customers to ensure clear and open communication, especially during the buildup and teardown. Recommend looking into the possibility of purchasing cellular phones that are compatible with the service provided overseas for each contingency kit.

4. *Evaluation of Agreements and Operating Procedures*

   a. *Host Nation Agreements* (impact on contingency contracting)

      i. Host Nation Support: (Host nation support agreements in place how to get a copy, U.S. Embassy information—contact information—POCs—availability, Other U.S. and Allied Nation military installations in the area supported—available)

      ii. Host Nation Issues: (Specifics about what contracts host nation controls such as fuel, travel restrictions—Threats—Host Nation Emergency info, hospitals, emergency services—Language problems—Political impediments—Customs and Tariffs—Weather—Location Geography—)

iii. *Host Nation Customs:* (anything other COs should be aware of such as holidays and their impact on the Contingency Contracting role, behavior which could be offensive to locals, courtesies which need to be observed, business practices like bribery, nothing open after 3 p.m., religious issues)

    b. *Status of Forces Agreements* (impact on contingency contracting)

    c. *OPLAN* (adequacy)

    d. *Training*

5. *Issues Affecting Contracting Process:* This section should contain insight into obstacles in completing your contracting mission. For example, funding problems, currency problems, security issues, language barriers, supply and labor shortages, warrant problems, delays attributed to hostile actions, etc.

    Problems encountered with the Contracting Process. _____ is an Islamic nation and observes all the customs and holidays as such. The workweek is Saturday through Wednesday with the weekend being Thursday and Friday. Many of the businesses are open on Thursday but all are closed on Friday. Business hours are normally 0800–1200 in the morning with a lunch break between 1200–1600 and 1600–2000 in the evening. Catering, refuse, custodial, and sewage worked on the weekend due to the existing BPAs.

    Obtaining passes onto the installation for contractors was extremely difficult. All pass information had to be routed through the _____ security police. Operations in the AOR are much different than in the States and most of the contractors had to rely on those whom they knew in order to obtain a pass. Some of the apparent low bidders on some of our contracts did not start work for two weeks while others obtained a pass in minutes and started work immediately. Contracts were not awarded with enough lead time to allow the contractors to obtain passes. This resulted in having to use the contractors with passes until the apparent low bidder could obtain a pass.

Customers provided inadequate item descriptions. Terminology in the deployed location is not the same as in the U.S. For example, they use the metric system. In addition, many hours were wasted trying to locate customers in order to find out exactly what was needed. In order to minimize the item description problems a contracting individual was available to quality check each individual AF Form 9 (purchase request) as they were turned in to Contracting.

Military Popular Writing: Magazines and Journals

Just as most institutions of higher education sponsor student publications such as campus newspapers, undergraduate research journals, and literary magazines, many military units produce and distribute similar publications. These publications offer military personnel (such as the young Air Force Lieutenant Tom Moncure, whose 1975 article published in the Strategic Air Command's magazine Combat Crew *appears below) a venue in which to present their critical and creative work (see the sidebar call for a "top-notch cartoonist-illustrator" to serve as the art editor for* Combat Crew*).*

This exchange is an example using banter as feedback that student veterans may initially engage in during a peer review session

Here Moncure demonstrates close reading of a military manual

The description of flight maps as "works of art" is characteristic of military humor

LT. THOMAS B. MONCURE
51 Bomb Sq, Seymour Johnson AFB

"You actually chose a B-52 over an IP assignment?"

"I don't know about you, but I wouldn't fly any aircraft that doesn't do aero."

"You'll only log copilot time, and wait years to be an aircraft commander."

Such is a sample of the feedback one sometimes gets when he chooses a "heavy" or "many motor" at the end of UPT these days. Granted there are certain thrills that only the T-38 (White Rocket) can give. For personal reasons, being a pilot training instructor did not attract me too much, so I took a B-52 assignment to Seymour Johnson AFB in North Carolina, close to my Virginia home.

After an enjoyable week at Carswell AFB, Texas, for Weapons School, and a miserable two weeks at Fairchild AFB, Washington, for Survival School, I arrived at Castle AFB, California for the four-month B-52 course. As academics started, my worst fears seemed to be coming true. I thought, "Is the copilot just a check-list reader . . . a glorified secretary?" The information to be learned seemed endless, and I had yet to start flying the thing. A little sentence in section eight of the Dash One seemed to describe what I thought my job would be for the next several years, it read ". . . he (the copilot) will also act as flight engineer."

With a swirling head full of knowledge received from the academic section, I trundled myself down to the flight line and began what is now nearly a year of flying the BUF. Naturally, my experience is limited, and I am not an authority on life in SAC, alert, or the combat crew business. On the other hand, I have been through enough B-52 training missions to know the copilot is much more than a checklist reader. Indeed he is one-sixth of a crew, and his proficiency (or lack of it) can easily determine the success of the mission, not to mention the safety of the aircraft.

Beginning with mission planning, one finds the copilot completing all calculations relating to the performance of the aircraft. Takeoff data, weight and balance, and the fuel log all must be computed and checked. Errors in aircraft performance data can cause a flight to be unsafe indeed. Missions average nine hours so miscalculations in the fuel log could result in lost training and if not identified in time, dangerously low fuel. Incorrect takeoff data might mean an unnecessarily aborted takeoff which would make you unpopular with everybody from the wing commander down. Drawing maps and keeping them current is also a part of mission planning for the copilot, who cross-checks his works of art closely with the navigator for accuracy. Low

level at night in the weather is no time to argue about the heading and altitude for the next leg. Being able to dei all of the above quickly and with great accuracy is of prime importance for the copilot, especially in the face of rapidly chang-. ing weather or mission profiles.

Arriving at the aircraft an hour and a half prior to flight, the copilot finds that he has a lot more to do than just the paperwork. He does half of the exterior inspection and must be . as capable of verifying aircraft condition for there is no backup for this inspection. Once inside the aircraft, the same holds true for the inspections and opera-tional checks of many important aircraft systems which are on the copilot's side of the cockpit and out of the pilot's reach.

From takeoff to engine shutdown, the "co" Makes sure the aircraft and crew functions smoothly and efficiently, foreseeing potential problems and making sure they do not become serious, or in many cases, even materialize in the first place. During normal operations, the co-pilot controls the radios, runs the extensive check-list, maintains the fuel log, and monitors the air-craft position, all the while frequently checking flight instruments and advising the pilot of any significant deviations. This constant "keeping on top of things" makes the aircraft and crew all the more capable of completing the assigned mission, which is what it is all about.

Occasionally I miss the yanking and banking of fighter-type aircraft. The B-52 offers its own thrills; however, such as low level, refueling, and it's great being able to move around a little inside the plane. The precision required to keep a bird the size of the BUF under control when in close proximity to the ground or another aircraft is considerable. Also, pilots are faced with many changing control responses and trim requirements during the course of a mission due to gross weight and configuration changes. (The BUF can weigh anywhere between 180,000 and 488,000 pounds in-flight, depending on fuel load alone.) The most often heard complaint is probably about the nine to ten hour missions for which little can be done, because once low level, re-fueling, a nav leg, and some pattern work are added together, the total is seldom less than eight hours.

In the air, there is plenty of opportunity for the copilot to hand-fly the aircraft. While it is true that the aircraft must be on autopilot for the nav leg, and the pilot usually does the refueling, most pilots will readily transfer control during other times and assume the copilot's duties. It doesn't pay for a copilot to be content not flying the aircraft and just reading the checklist and managing systems. That leads to sloppy instrument flying which hurts at upgrade time. I enjoy simply flying the climbs, descents, or any-time I can pass my paperwork to the boss in favor of handling the aircraft. This way, it is easier to remind myself, "your aeronautical rating is pilot, your crew position is temporarily co-pilot."

All of this is reducible to the simple fact that although being a B-52 copilot is not all fun, there is no less a necessity for a very professional job through the entire mission. I find satisfaction in the fact that I can fly an aircraft unlike any other, for while there are several fighter-types, transports, and such available to pilots today, there is only one BUF and it offers a very valuable experience.

OCTOBER 1975

Are you a top notch cartoonist-illustrator? Here's an opportunity to prove it as you ex-pand your horizons!

The interesting and challenging position of Art Editor, Combat Crew, is now open to the airman that qualifies. If you would like to try for the position and work with a professional magazine staff, send examples of your cartoon-ing illustrations to Editor, Combat Crew, Offutt AFB, NE, 68113. Do it now! The position never stays open long!!

Veteran writers will be used to incorporating jargon into their texts

3

Transferring Veteran Knowledge

IN SEPTEMBER 2010, NEARLY A decade after the terrorist attacks in the United States that would lead to the wars in Afghanistan and Iraq, John Schupp was awarded the Zachary and Elizabeth Fisher Distinguished Civilian Humanitarian Award by the Department of Defense (DoD). Schupp, a chemistry professor at Cleveland State University, received the award for creating SERV (Supportive Education for the Returning Veteran), an innovative program aimed at helping former members of the Armed Forces make the transition from military service to college life. The Fisher Award recognizes individuals whose work best exemplifies the humanitarian ideals of the DoD, and SERV was widely promoted as an effective model for helping former service members adjust to their civilian lives in college communities—communities that can often feel foreign to veterans, particularly those who are returning from combat or from a theater of war. The structure of college, which often lacks clear hierarchies or easily navigable support systems, paired with a population of nonveteran students who may have little understanding of service in war (Alvarez; DiRamio; Rumann and Hamrick; *Military-Civilian Gap;* Elliott, Gonzalez, and Larsen; Naphan and Elliot), frequently results in disorienting transitions for veterans as they move from military to civilian life. This disorientation often occurs because student veterans must confront a dramatic shift from a lifestyle in which "authority is absolute, responsibility for actions lies in the hands of superiors and . . . the rules are clear" (Zinger and Cohen 39–40) to a less hierarchal system present in many colleges. In other words, as a 2008 article in the *New York Times* pointed out, "veterans step into college life from a highly structured system and are bedeviled by the looseness they find" (Alvarez). While student veterans generally intend to be highly focused on their new "mission" to obtain a college degree,[1] they often become frustrated by the complexities of negotiating the unfamiliar administrative, academic, and cultural structures of higher education, and thus may lose focus on their primary goal or drop out of college altogether.

Schupp's belief that "adjusting to the college environment, in general, often is the most difficult part of the transition from military life" (Carden)[2] generated his desire to create SERV, and his programming received significant coverage in both the popular media and in military and academic circles. For example, the *San Diego Union-Tribune* described Schupp's cohort model as "life-changing" (Barr), the Armed Forces Press Service touted the fact that "[u]niversities and colleges and Veterans Affairs systems across the country" took an interest in Schupp's programming (Carden), and the *Chronicle of Higher Education* lauded Schupp for his persistence and his drive to "overcome institutional inertia" to get the program started (Field, "As Congress"). Consequently, Schupp's became a central voice that recommended educators and administrators look closely at not only the challenges student veterans face adjusting to life on college campuses, but also the benefits of increasing student veteran enrollment and retention for institutions of higher education.

Such national discussions about veterans' "transition" (singular) to college have subsequently proven valuable in guiding initiatives for recruiting and retaining student veterans. For example, an increasing number of colleges are hiring veterans resource officers to help students negotiate unfamiliar academic structures as well as institutional and Veterans Administration (VA) bureaucracies, and these veterans-services personnel are increasingly housed in designated veterans' centers—spaces on campus where student veterans can congregate to socialize, study, and support one another and that serve as "one-stop shops" for connecting student veterans to campus and community resources. Some colleges offer veterans-only courses (see Chapter 4) or specific student veteran orientations, and several offer priority course registration for veterans.[3]

Many institutions have supported and encouraged the formation of local chapters of the Student Veterans of America (SVA),[4] and some have held veterans' awareness weeks or sponsored programs and speakers related to veterans' issues in an attempt to bridge the "military-civilian gap." These initiatives, and many others like them, aim to facilitate student veterans' adjustment to university life and help decrease their feelings of alienation and/or isolation on college campuses. Underlying many of these initiatives is the assumption that most veterans experience a single transition from service member to college student. For instance, Columbia University declares that it "launched the Center for Veteran Transition and Integration to have a direct and lasting impact on the issue of veteran transition and upward mobility by creating and providing access to the best-in-class tools and programming veterans need as they transition from active service to college and the workforce" (*Center*). Along the same lines, Oregon State University's student newspaper features a story that acknowledges that "[m]any veterans face a difficult transition to college life," and declares that "Oregon State's veteran resource programs are doing everything in their power to make that adjustment easier on veterans" (Kalama).

A similar assumption regarding veterans undergoing a singular transition can be found in the materials that the DoD Transition Assistance Program (TAP) provides to service members separating from the military. Over the course of a well-meaning but often insufficient five-day workshop, TAP provides guidance to assist service members to "make the initial transition from military service to the civilian workplace" ("Transition Assistance"). Although the face-to-face TAP workshop primarily focuses on preparing active duty service members to make the transition to veteran status, to access and understand their benefits, and to enter the civilian workforce, participants can opt to attend an additional two-day "Accessing Higher Education" workshop intended to assist them in "identifying the higher education requirements that support their personal career goals. The two-day workshop is divided into four topic areas: choosing a program of study, selecting an institution of higher education, exploring funding sources, and navigating the admission process" ("Training Tracks"). While these higher education–focused workshops undoubtedly provide some relevant materials and basic information regarding the college application process, course selection, and financial aid, they cannot help but be cursory and oversimplified. Not surprisingly, despite the workshop's stated outcome that each participant "will create a customized plan for a successful transition to a higher education institution" ("508"), student veterans often lament "the lack of preparation they felt they received as they transitioned out of the military" (Olsen, Badger, and McCuddy 106).

Furthermore, the various ways that student veterans are actually pursuing their postservice educational goals suggest a different dynamic than simply a singular "transition" in terms of the academic pathways they follow, let alone with respect to their personal lives. Indeed, many veterans who choose to earn a bachelor's degree first enroll in either online or community colleges. In some cases, they may begin their coursework with outreach education programs offered on military bases before they move on to a four-year college. According to a 2009 report by the American Council on Education (ACE), "A plurality (43 percent) of military undergraduates in 2007–08 attended public two-year institutions" (Radford vi). Five years later, the Student Veterans of America Million Records Project approximated that "nearly half of the sample (48.5 percent) [of student veterans they surveyed] first earned an associate-level degree" (Cate 36–37) before seeking a four-year degree.[5] And Curt Aasen, the director of institutional effectiveness at Tidewater Community College in Norfolk, Virginia, has estimated that nearly 60 percent of Tidewater's student veterans transfer with the intention of finishing somewhere else, with or without having obtained associate's degrees or other credentials (Marcus).[6]

The key point here is that for many student veterans, their transition is not simply a single one from the military to college. Instead, the numbers suggest that a significant percentage of the veterans who matriculate at four-year colleges, in particular, have already attended and most likely been successful students at community colleges. Therefore, their initial transition from military service member to civilian student frequently occurs in a two-year college setting, where they have far more agency in determining their course schedules and are far more likely to find a similar peer group in terms of age, personal lives,[7] and educational agendas.[8] It is in that transitional setting, therefore, that many student veterans develop an initial conception of what college is and what is expected of them as students. When they move to a four-year college and are confronted with a dramatically different educational setting—one that very often includes the expectation that they will join a new culture and identify themselves with a very specific institutional climate with a more "traditional" undergraduate student demographic[9]—veterans may find themselves feeling disconnected not just from their prior military experiences, but also from the academic experiences and interpersonal skills that they acquired as students in community colleges.

We suggest that these circumstances point to a significant problem: what is frequently portrayed as a single transition from the military to college is in fact far more complicated, even just in terms of educational variations (not to mention adjustments in personal lives, work lives, financial situations, etc.). Veterans who move from community colleges to four-year institutions face not just one, but at least two educational transitions. As Brandy Jenner has argued, student veterans are not merely exiting their roles as active service members. As she explains, "Role exit, though a useful contribution to identity transition theory, is problematic because it collapses the myriad transitions student veterans undergo and fails to account for multiple simultaneous transitions." Such failure to account for the dissonance among these simultaneous and subsequent transitions requires us to rethink how to approach the notion of a veteran's educational "transition" altogether, as, first, the transition from service member to student, typically in a community college or online venue, and, second, the transition from community college student to four-year university student. This second transition has remained largely invisible in scholarship on student veterans, yet we argue that it may be as important as the first. Indeed, we suggest that the invisibility of this second transition may in part account for some of the attrition of veterans from the academy. We propose that thinking of multiple transitions even within a university system is especially important for student veterans, and we propose that writing classrooms can provide an especially useful location for intervention. Additionally, we argue that due to the focus on a singular "transition," educators miss opportunities to facilitate the shift from military workplace to college campus.

THE LIMITS OF THE SCHOLARSHIP ON MILITARY TRANSITIONS AND THE NEED FOR A TRANSFER FOCUS

The concept of transition dominates much of the scholarship surrounding student veterans (DiRamio, Ackerman, and Mitchell; Ryan et al.; Jones, "Understanding Student Veterans" and "Understanding Transition"; Griffin and Gilbert; Gregg, Howell, and Shordike). We acknowledge that this research on veterans' transitions into higher education is vitally important for postsecondary educational institutions to consider because military veterans constitute a distinctive and potentially vulnerable student population (Steele, Salcedo, and Coley 1). That vulnerability, however, points to limits surrounding the notion of transition and suggests the need for a different model. The concept of "transition" often presumes a fundamental shift in the identity of the person undergoing the transition. It typically also carries with it a significant expectation of change. The student veteran is expected to put aside military habits of mind, attitudes, and conduct and adopt civilian ones instead. The assumption seems to be that in order to "transition" from service members to civilians, veterans will have to retool themselves in order to function successfully as college students. For example, "in military environments, unit members often share a close bond as they spend large amounts of time together in high-stress situations" (Olsen, Badger, and McCuddy 104), yet in many college classes, the emphasis is placed on individual effort.[10] As Lim et al. explain, the culture of higher education privileges "a set of values and priorities, such as competitiveness, individualism, personal responsibility, and independent thinking that often conflicts with military values"

(293). While such a focus on self-reliance may resonate with many individuals who separate from military service,[11] it also requires a willingness to "leave behind" one set of values and practices in order to embrace a new one, a notion that is understandably disconcerting.

As Lim et al. point out, "Schlossberg's transition model has been widely used as the leading theoretical framework" for studying military to civilian transitions (294). Nancy Schlossberg defines a transition as "an event or non-event [that] results in a change in assumptions about oneself and the world and thus requires a corresponding change in behaviors and relationships" (5). Lim and her colleagues developed a cyclical model of adult transition articulated as "Moving In, Moving Through, Moving Out." However, assuming that student veterans will "move out" of their military service member identity as they "move in" to their civilian student identity, the model overlooks the reality that veterans have amassed considerable life and educational experiences that can, if reoriented, enrich their return to civilian communities. As Sue Doe and William Doe explain, "Leaving the military, in other words, does not have to mean that the military person must wipe clean his or her identities but rather that military experience and its attendant literacies can be understood as valuable influences upon the way the veteran thinks and acts in new contexts." Instead of transitioning away from the military, which might carry with it an expectation of "starting over, regardless of what one [has] accomplished in the service, which [is] often demoralizing" (Naphan and Elliot 44), we argue that veterans may be better served by learning to carry over their relevant military experiences into the civilian world.

Student veterans in particular are likely to benefit from learning to see connections between their military and academic lives. We propose that rather than seeing their objective as transition, student veterans may benefit from understanding their objective as transfer—a transfer of a skill set, work experience, and/or life experience from one community or workplace to another. In other words, instead of *transition*—a term that carries with it a sense of leaving behind their previous identities as service members—*trans-*

fer promotes the idea that student veterans can import their experiences and situate them in new contexts. Embracing the concept of transfer and being intentional about helping student veterans to facilitate that transfer reorients the veteran experience as part of a continuum of educational experiences that simply occurred in different contexts. It encourages veterans to forge connections and see their military identities as formative of their civilian educational goals. We acknowledge Mark Blaauw-Hara's point that student veterans'

> ability to fluidly transfer their writing skills to the classroom is complicated by the fact that the writing they did in the military was bound up in the larger practices and learning environment of the armed forces. They know, for example, how to write an effective evaluation of a subordinate, but they may have trouble abstracting the skills of clarity, directness, and evidence and applying them to academic writing because the military and academic environments are so different. ("Learning")

However, as Corinne Hinton argues, "[a] student who believes that his or her prior knowledge is valuable to current contexts is more likely to use those experiences or knowledge in the building of new knowledge[12] *but generally only when prompted or guided to do so*" (emphasis added).[13] For example,

> The Marine student veterans [in Hinton's study] who were able to identify and then translate previous learning and rhetorical experiences from the military into academic writing contexts reported positive perceptions about that writing" and "shared many ways in which their previous experiences and knowledge with military writing assisted them in their academic writing development across the disciplines. ("Military")[14]

Perhaps in part because writing is considered both an applied or practical "skill" as well as a valid academic discipline, writing classrooms provide an especially useful place for student veterans to learn the value of transfer as a mode of education. Additionally, since writing instructors often teach general education courses that can be satisfied at least in part online or at community colleges, and because many four-year institutions require transfer students to enroll in designated transfer student writing courses, writing instructors may often see firsthand student veterans grappling with two (or more) educational transitions. They are likely to see the ways that the student veterans negotiate those transitions, and their classrooms are likely to be the site of some of the complex interactions that result from a service member trying to grapple not just with differences between the military and college, but also between one type of college culture and another. We propose that as witnesses to those transitions, writing instructors are especially well positioned to help veterans transfer their previous experiences to new educational contexts. In doing so, they can assist veterans who desire to retain relevant strengths of their military identities[15] while they are simultaneously in the process of adopting their student identities.[16] Instead of expecting them to "transition" out of their military identity, in other words, the expectation becomes that writing instructors "prompt and guide" (Hinton, "Military") student veterans to "transfer" the benefits and recognize the limits of their military learning habits and writing experiences.

THE FIRST TRANSITION: TWO-YEAR COLLEGES, ADJUSTMENT, AND STASIS

Any generalization about either student veterans or types of institutions of higher education necessarily draws lines that are not fully inclusive. Even so, certain traits appear with some regularity and provide a useful framework for understanding how and why two-year colleges constitute the first transition from military service to civilian life for many student veterans. By understanding that initial educational transition, writing instructors may be better equipped to facilitate the second transition—a transition that may actually be starker and more pronounced than the first—and may even be better able to reorient their approach to student veterans from a theory of transition toward a theory of transfer.

As discussed previously in this chapter, two-year colleges offer an attractive entrée into higher education for veterans for many of the same reasons that other "nontraditional" students find them attractive: "low tuition, convenient location [close to work and family], flexible scheduling, an open-door admissions policy, and programs and services designed to support at-risk students" (Calcagno et al. 632). Jones goes so far as to suggest that "[b]ecause of their high percentage of veteran students, their ability to offer targeted courses and services, and their historically special relationship with the communities they serve, *community colleges are at the vanguard of student-veteran transition*" ("Understanding Student Veterans" 3, emphasis added).

Heightening the attractiveness is the fact that enrollment in two-year colleges does not often carry with it an expectation that students will enculturate into an on-campus community. At many two-year colleges, just as with many online courses, veterans (as well as other "nontraditional" students) may be minimally involved in a campus culture. For example, Kristin Wilson et al. found that the student veterans they interviewed "appeared to have little to no interest in traditional aspects of college, like athletics, social groups, or campus activities" (635).[17] In fact, older students in general "spend less time on campus and are thus less involved in extracurricular activities compared with their younger peers"; however, these same students "are more engaged in classroom-based activities" (Schwehm 11), and David Vacchi and Joseph Berger discovered that "*[a]cademic integration* with a campus is more prominent in the success of nontraditional students such as veterans due to a diminished need to adapt socially to campus" (126, emphasis added).

Because of the structure of academic classes at two-year colleges, veterans are likely to benefit from beginning their civilian higher education there. First of all, two-year colleges have a higher concentration of adult learners than do traditional colleges,[18] and many of those adult learners will be returning to schooling after a hiatus of six or more years, an academic "gap" shared by most student veterans. Paired with the shared experience of the demands of working full-time in a career, along with the greater likelihood of being a spouse and/or a parent, student veterans are more likely to establish a level of comfort and connection between themselves and older civilian students attending community colleges. For example, Brian Gregg, Dana Howell, and Anne Shordike discovered that "[a]s veterans found others to empathize with their current life circumstances, they reported being more connected with the university" (6). While civilian adult learners may not share in the types of military experiences that veterans bring with them, they do in many cases share similar reasons for pursuing an education and motivations for seeking a degree. As Olusegun Agboola Sogunro points out, "Generally, adult learners perceive learning as a means to an end and, therefore, value learning experiences only if they are relevant and applicable to their needs" (29). Similarly, student veterans "view college as a bridge between the military and the workforce. After leaving the military [veterans enroll in college seeking] meaningful credentials that will ensure that their transition into the workforce in the field of their choosing is successful" (Wilson 57), a point that reflects our discussion of the genesis of the GI Bill in Chapter 2. These points of contact suggest possibilities for easing transition. For those veterans who are more fully involved in their workplaces or who may be negotiating the demands of disability, mental health, or family challenges, the two-year college represents an opportunity for educational advancement that can be completed around their own schedules. For those who choose full-time study at the community college, a classroom with a greater percentage of students who more closely resemble them in age, maturity, and lifestyle[19] likely mitigates some of the sense of alienation veterans often report at four-year colleges, where most of the other full-time students are more likely to be "traditional" straight-out-of-high-school types.

In addition, two-year institutions often have "smaller class sizes, more direct faculty-student interaction, and [the] ability to offer courses and an environment that cater to adult and nontraditional students" (Jones, "Understanding Transition" 109). As Holly Wheeler discovered in her interviews with student veterans, several of those who chose to attend two-year colleges did so because they "appreciated being able to ask for extra help and having professors available outside of class, a service [one interviewee] reported his friends at four-year institutions 'just don't have'" (780). Two-year colleges, then, may function as transitional spaces that provide veterans with a less jarring adjustment to student life. In addition,

> for student veterans who are initially uncertain about how successful they may be academically,[20] earning an Associate's degree can give them the confidence to continue to a Bachelor's degree. Well-established articulation agreements between many state two- and four-year colleges make such transfers particularly viable options.[21] (Hart and Thompson, "Veterans in the Writing Classroom" 349)

However, there remain potential points of conflict for those veterans who make the second transition to four-year colleges.

THE SECOND TRANSITION: FOUR-YEAR COLLEGES AND CAMPUS ENCULTURATION

Taken as a whole, research suggests that a student veteran's adjustment to the academic rigor necessary to earn a bachelor's degree is minimal in comparison to the difficulty in enculturating to a more "traditional" college campus. Certainly, academic challenges may remain a hurdle for some student veterans, such as those Di-Ramio, Ackerman, and Mitchell interviewed who acknowledged that they were experiencing difficulties due to "[p]oor study habits and lack of focus" ("From Combat" 87). However, the research indicates that work habits and dedication to academic study tend not to be the primary challenge for student veterans. For example, student veterans often describe "the work ethic and time management skills that were a part of military life [as] strong assets in an academic setting" resulting in their habits of "attending each class on time, meeting deadlines for assignments and papers, preparing adequately for upcoming exams, and coordinating plans with peers for group assignments" (Olsen, Badger, and McCuddy 103–04).[22] The real issue in the transition, then, is helping veterans reorient from both a military culture where their work habits were formed and a community college experience where they could complete much of their work in an environment that required little in terms of social integration. As Kristin Wilson et al. explain, "Academic integration is seen as a function of student academic performance and academic interactions with college faculty and staff, whereas social integration is seen as formal and informal involvement with peers, faculty, and extracurricular activities" (629). As we noted earlier, few student veterans tend to become engaged with extracurricular activities or social events on campus, in part due to "unpleasant or intrusive interactions with civilian peers,[23] who may convey little knowledge or concern about the current conflicts overseas, ask inappropriate questions (e.g., if s/he had killed someone while deployed), or express a lack of military appreciation (e.g., lack of observance of Veterans Day)," resulting in a situation in which it becomes "uncomfortable or unappealing [for student veterans] to integrate into the typical student lifestyle" (Borsari et al. 167). Yet for many "traditional" undergraduates at four-year colleges, participating in the "typical student lifestyle" is one of the most appealing aspects of their college experience. Unlike these traditional students, who,

> as Caroline Bird suggested during the post-Vietnam [enrollment] surge, frequently attend college "because it has become the thing to do or because college is a pleasant place to be; because it's the only way they can get parents or taxpayers to support them without getting a job they don't like," student-veterans expect institutions of higher education to be more than "a social center or aging vat." Instead, many seek accelerated entry into a productive and sustainable economic life. (Hart and Thompson, "Veterans in the Writing Classroom" 349)

TRANSFER TRUMPS TRANSITION

Because the number of transitions veterans endure are both difficult to generalize and multifaceted in individual lives, a shift of discussion from "transition" to "transfer" provides veterans with more clearly articulated points of contact between their military lives and their lives as civilian students. Further, embracing "transfer" as a core concept allows student veterans to forgo any expectation that they will have to "lose" or let go of their military identities. Instead, they learn to see both the opportunities and the limits of their military identities and training in order to carry over the productive elements into the new setting of higher education.

Transfer has also emerged as an important concept in writing studies and attendant fields. Emerging out of linguistics, its migration to WS more generally has been fostered by faculty and researcher attempts to understand precisely what carries over from classroom writing instruction to other courses and even the workplace. The goal has been to ensure that writing pedagogy connects student writing assigned in courses to other contexts, and the study of transfer has emerged within the rhetorical context of university curricula. Indeed, as Jenn Fishman and Mary Jo Reiff, Stephanie Boone et al., and Kathleen Blake Yancey, Liane Robertson and Kara Taczak have all demonstrated, transfer can be used to frame entire course sequences to ensure that students understand the relationship among different courses.

At the heart of transfer research is the idea that knowledge uptake occurs as a process that builds upon previously established skills, experience, and wisdom. Instead of seeing learning as regulated by confrontation with entirely new ideas or activity, transfer imagines learning as something akin to a process of analogy, whereby students intuitively take in new information within frameworks that are already familiar to them. Learning, in this formulation, means building upon previous foundations and applying previous systems to novel situations—even situations that require a complete overhaul or revision of previous models and systems.

Educational systems that embrace transfer models take it as their goal to facilitate students' abilities to make connections between older skill sets and knowledge and newer ones, encouraging students to forge relationships between ideas in order to see them not only within disciplinary and cultural contexts, but within the context of their own educational histories and personal lives (see Eodice, Geller, and Lerner). Educational approaches built on transfer thus present learning as an ongoing and expanding set of relationships that students construct as a kind of knowledge architecture in their lives.

David Perkins and Gavriel Salomon have been frequent champions of transfer as a goal of educational practices. Seeing transfer as already implicit in many curricula, they argue that the best models of education are more intentional in their use of transfer. Advocating for what they call the "Good Shepherd" theory, they envision educators as shepherds who help students see not only that their learning may be applicable to more than one field of practice, but also that the process by which they learn can also be used to maximize their own accretion of wisdom and skills ("Science and Art").

Within writing studies, Anne Beaufort and Rebecca Nowacek have been primary advocates for the idea of transfer as a cornerstone of writing pedagogy. Both Beaufort and Nowacek advance arguments based primarily on qualitative methods (with Beaufort relying on writing ethnographies of students) in order to posit transfer as generative of effective writing instruction. For Beaufort, writing instruction is carried on within a lineage of social and cultural constructs that shape student perceptions and behaviors. According to Beaufort, an effective instructor makes the various components of students' writerly histories transparent by providing students with ways of discerning differences in contexts. Specifically, she believes teachers should help students parse the domains of writing process knowledge, subject matter knowledge, rhetorical knowledge, and genre knowledge in order to help them understand precisely how they are learning and how best to carry over ideas from one domain to another.

Nowacek's research is more expansive in both aims and execution. She argues that transfer is a "rhetorical act," and as such cannot only be taught, but can also be used by faculty as pedagogy. Further, she argues that transfer is especially complex, and that when learning transfer, students and faculty face together extensive and complicated institutional structures that, on the one hand, foster the idea of transfer, while on the other hand, limit possibilities of actualizing transfer processes. Nowacek's romantic vision of the university as an especially vibrant place for transfer is compelling, even if some critics, like Amy Devitt, might argue with her more expansive view of transfer as a rhetorical act applicable across a wide range of institutional structures.[24]

Nowacek's work is especially helpful to consider for researchers working in veterans studies. Because her work self-consciously focuses on institutional frameworks, it fits particularly well with imagining how writing studies and veterans studies intersect within the context of a university. For example, as Michelle Navarre Cleary and Kathryn Wozniak point out, "While most adult students come to composition classes appreciating the importance of clear writing, they often do not understand how or why they need to know how to write academic essays. Likewise, veterans can be confounded by the differences between military and academic writing expectations." By focusing their writing pedagogy on transfer, by helping student veterans to see "both the differences (such as the need to develop support for claims) as well as the similarities (such as the value of concise wording) between their military and academic writing" and reminding "veterans who are struggling with the 'foreignness' of academic writing that they have already become proficient in specialized discourse communities" (Navarre Cleary and Wozniak), writing instructors can help student veterans mitigate that confusion and frustration.

The examples provided in Writing/Practices 1 in this volume demonstrate the proficiency that student veterans have with a variety of rhetorical tasks in a variety of writing genres. Helping veterans transfer the lessons of those rhetorical moves and genres provides a framework within which they can scale their new rhetorical situations. Put another way, military writing experiences, despite their highly standardized forms, are rhetorical constructions latent with lessons about genre, audience, purpose, and occasion, and any failure to recognize that is likely less about student inability and more about instructor engagement. Just as any student comes to a class with preconceived notions of what constitutes "good writing," so too do many service members. The difference is that veterans' knowledge of forms of writing is typically forged in real-world circumstances with high-stakes outcomes that are foreign to many first-year writing instructors. In other words, many veterans come with significant and powerful writing experiences from their time in service, and as a result they carry with them writing strategies that may be more advanced, even if more situated within a non-academic context, than those of first-year writers just coming from high school into college. Indeed, veterans may bring with them writing strategies that have direct, real-world impact—on their careers, on their promotions, on the safety of their fellow service members, or on the lives of those in combat zones.

TRANSFER PRINCIPLES FOR STUDENT VETERANS IN THE WRITING CLASSROOM

Principle 1: De-escalation of Writing Stakes May Be Necessary for Student Veterans

The task of transfer for student veterans may be one of de-escalation. Certainly, many lower-stakes writing tasks exist in the vast bureaucracy of the American military. Yet there remains among many military veterans the sense that each one of their acts contributes to a greater purpose or mission, and that each action has compounding effects as it moves up the chain of command. With that realization comes a sense of duty and obligation that, while one that many of us might wish our students to have, in fact bears little resemblance to the potential outcomes of most first-year writing assignments. Student veterans may consider such assignments to be a greater burden simply because much of the writing in their professional lives led more immediately to significant and/or concrete results. Helping student veterans recontextualize the outcomes of these assignments as developing facility with a writing process and habit of mind that can withstand risks and can generate new ideas, not simply reflect the needs of or obligations to others, is part of the task of transfer, and while most veterans are keenly aware of the ways that their college education may seem "fuzzy" and less concrete in its aims and methods compared to their training in the service, few will likely have given much thought to how that plays out in something like their writing habits. A faculty member's job, then, becomes demonstrating that though the context for writing has changed, the sense that, as Richard Weaver once insisted, "any utterance is a major assumption of responsibility" (6) has not.

Principle 2: Help Student Veteran Writers Recognize the Explicitly Audience-Focused Genres by Which They Communicated in the Military

Communication within the military, especially for formal written documents and presentations, is notoriously succinct and purpose-driven. Its aim is often direct action. Veterans, however, may not recognize how important audience as a concept is to their communication. Because most military members are taught rigid genres for written expression or are simply taught to respond in highly stylized and extraordinarily constrained ways when communicating orally, the audience of the communication may not be explicitly discussed as such. Even so, once attention has been drawn to the role of the audience, student veterans will likely see the impact it has had on their modes of expression while in the service. They will likely recognize that their response to a higher-ranking officer was different from their response to a similarly ranked enlisted colleague, and that can help them realize that the styles, modes, and genres of military expression carry within them highly choreographed and deployed markers for audience. Once audience is clarified as central to communication within the service, even if it is sometimes obfuscated by highly controlled genres, students may have greater appreciation for its role outside the military as well.

Chapter 3 Implementation Questions

- Does your campus provide targeted support for student veterans' movement from either the military to community college or from community college to a four-year institution?
- What other kinds of transitions might student veterans face when matriculating to your institution—transitions that may be unique to your campus or student body?

- Does your curriculum explicitly orient students to the difference between low-stake assignments and higher-stake ones?
- How can you illustrate to students that even if a writing assignment is low stakes, it carries with it important implications about larger writing concepts and processes?
- Which assignments in your course aim explicitly to develop a sense of audience and how can they be crafted to draw attention to ways that genre itself is linked to audience?

4

Developing Veteran-Informed Classrooms

SINCE AT LEAST 2003, AS WE NOTED earlier, veteran enrollments in core courses such as first-year writing (FYW) have spiked.[1] Because FYW courses are typically small enough for students to interact one on one with their instructors and to collaborate with their classmates,[2] and because expressive and reflective writing theories shape many first-year students' writing experiences,[3] writing classes often function as a transitional space between a veteran's military experiences and their college experiences.

Sue Doe and William Doe have termed this transitional time for service members "residence time." They describe "residence time" as the amount of time it takes for a person to become fully acclimated to a new environment, and they call on the concept of "induction" as the process by which veterans make the transition into residence time. For Doe and Doe, veterans, in moving from military life to civilian life, may experience a more extended period of "induction" than during their original transition into the military, and so the goal of educators should be, at least in part, to reduce the length of "residence time" through close attention to the varied literacies of military service members.

Residence time provides a useful framework for engaging with veterans on college campuses in that it emphasizes the sometimes extensive transitions veterans undergo (see Chapter 3). As we acknowledge in Chapter 1, not every institution or writing program will be affected by a veteran surge, but we nonetheless urge WPAs

An earlier version of this chapter was published in *College Composition and Communication*, vol. 68, no. 2, Dec. 2016, pp. 345–71.

to investigate veteran enrollments on their campuses to determine the degree to which these transitions may be taking place in their classrooms. Such a task is not easy. Very few colleges, if any, disclose veteran status to faculty,[4] so instructors often only become aware through veterans' self-disclosure as a result of classroom discussion, one-to-one conferences, informal or formal writing assignments, or, in some cases, discussion of accommodation for disability.[5] Absent such self-disclosure, many student veterans remain invisible, especially in classes populated by other adult learners.

Despite such invisibility, many colleges and universities have implemented courses to help student veterans reduce their residence time. Many of those courses take the form of early orientations to college that occur in the summer or skills-based (often no-credit) courses that aim to help student veterans prepare for coursework (e.g., test-taking strategies, note-taking strategies), connect with one another, and familiarize themselves with campus resources. However, alongside many of these "bridge" programs and/or orientation-type classes, writing programs have also piloted new types of courses that attempt to address the needs of veterans on campus.

Across the country three types of courses have, generally, been created to account for increases in military student populations: veterans-only courses, veteran-focused courses, and veteran-friendly courses. We provide below a taxonomy of these classes. While we focused our research on writing classrooms, these classifications also appear regularly in other disciplines and college orientation courses. Here, we trace the constituent parts of each category, but we also discuss governing assumptions behind each model and some of the theoretical architecture that supports those assumptions.

We would draw special attention to the fact that implementation of classes oriented to military audiences requires significant intellectual engagement with "the veteran" as a cultural trope or stereotype (see Vacchi). As we noted in the introduction to this volume, our culture has been saturated with the rhetoric of war for over a decade, forcing us to formulate our own positions about not only the wars, but also those who are sent to fight them. Confronting those positions, which are often forged in moments of intense emotion, is necessary to move ourselves and our classrooms beyond the essentializing language of the "hero," the "wounded warrior," the "war criminal," or other convenient categorizations.[6] New types of courses that aim to destigmatize veterans continue to emerge, and the categories of classes we describe below often foster more nuanced exploration of the connections between military service and academic inquiry.

VETERANS-ONLY COURSES

A sense of alienation among student veterans is well documented (see, for example, DiRamio, Ackerman, and Mitchell; Elliot, Gonzalez, and Larsen; Glasser, Powers, and Zywiak; and Livingston et al.), and the first category of classes—veterans-only classes—aims to remedy this estrangement by restricting course enrollment to veterans or members of the military. Such classes recognize the challenges that service members have in making transitions from military to civilian life, and they attempt to ease those transitions by ensuring that student veterans are surrounded by peers who understand military culture and the wartime service experience (see also Valentino, "Serving").

For veterans, a sense of "difference" can be heightened when they encounter student lives that seem fundamentally disconnected from their own lived experiences. In many of our interviews with students and faculty, the image of privileged undergraduate students who talk incessantly about their social lives emerged as a kind of trope, a stereotype against which many veterans positioned themselves. The stereotype served, in the veterans' minds, as evidence of the fundamental differences between the student veteran, who matured and was professionalized in a military (and often international) setting, and the "typical undergraduate," whose concerns focus on dating, alcohol, and parties.

Because (as Janet Lucas reminds us and as we discuss in Chapter 5) the writing classroom is a space where disclosures of life's personal details often emerge, this sense of difference can be exacerbated. Even in instances when instructors try to avoid prompting such disclosures, the use of experience as a type of evidence or as an organizing principle for a piece of writing may still lead to disclosure of a veteran's status. We note that even an assignment as seemingly innocuous as a "how-to" topic may unexpectedly reveal military experience. Writing professors who explicitly assign personal narratives increase such opportunities. In fact, our research suggests that, regardless of course goals, some form of personal narrative remains a mainstay of many composition classes.[7] As a result, the possibility that any particular student will disclose personal information that their classmates, the instructor, or even the student themself finds difficult to negotiate increases. For veterans, who already report a higher sense of alienation, personal writing may exacerbate those feelings, especially if their professors, as Melanie Burdick so openly discusses, find themselves unready for war stories and "afraid to respond" (354).

Veterans-only classes partly mitigate this issue because, on the one hand, faculty leading the class have typically received special preparation and, on the other hand, students share, at least broadly, a military context that can provide common touchstones for discussion and support. The model mirrors similar courses that have developed to aid other populations in higher education. Just as ESL or developmental writing sections of FYW seek to adapt shared learning objectives by acknowledging a need within the student population, so too do veterans-only writing courses. First popularized through the SERV program at Cleveland State University (see Chapter 3), the typical veterans-only course aims to provide a safe learning environment for veterans who may feel distracted or anxious in classes containing students without military backgrounds. SERV founder John Schupp found that veterans-only classes allow students to focus on their educational goals while finding support among peers. Classes that restrict enrollment to military veterans thus help the students establish a sense of "unit cohesion" that often allows them to focus more directly on the "mission" of class (Stripling). Such courses become "like the VFW hall without the alcohol," spaces where veterans "can talk about problems they may have, whether [they're] educational or personal" (Hall 8).

Several institutions have piloted veterans-only writing courses.

An instructor at a community college in a state with a significant military population created a veterans-only class that received national exposure in part because it recognized that the strong sense of camaraderie among service members could be harnessed as part of a writing class. As such, the initial class included trips to ropes courses and whitewater rafting to help create a strong learning cohort. The second semester of the course built on the lessons from the first and provided a shared reading experience on the subject of war. The course enjoyed significant success, but by the third semester it was offered, the instructor began to shift the focus away from the students' military experience because they found ongoing discussion about aspects of service and war at times frustrating and tedious. As a result, the instructor modified the course to focus on education and the college experience.

One professor at a regional comprehensive university in close proximity to a military base launched a veterans' learning community as part of her institution's introductory composition sequence. While debate about the desirability of the course emerged from discussions with student veterans, they nonetheless supported the pilot, which included service members from all the different branches. The approach was to provide "a space where if you want to write about service, it's a safe space," and while students reported some resistance to the writing process and to the "book learning" nature of the college setting, the instructor noted their ongoing strong sense of motivation and initiative.

Despite the many benefits reported from courses like the ones described above, they nonetheless present significant challenges, some pragmatic and some ethical. While the first institution discussed above continues to offer the veterans learning community FYW course in conjunction with a personal development course, the veterans-only course sequence at the latter institution was canceled in subsequent semesters, despite its relative success in achieving its goals (see Sura 189). At Cleveland State, the Veterans Student Success Program website shows that 2010 was the last year "SERV-only" English courses were offered, and an *Inside Higher Ed* article in 2012 reported that Cleveland State had discontinued the

SERV program entirely; a similar program at Ohio State was also discontinued (Grasgreen).

The relatively short history of veterans-only classes demonstrates that their viability often rests on issues of "logistics and demand": on the one hand, a class that is consistently underenrolled becomes unsustainable and a drain on limited resources, while, on the other hand, "a model based on one-on-one interactions and exceptionally small class sizes (which have to fit into everyone's schedules) can only reach so many people" (Grasgreen), so staffing veterans-only courses that are experiencing exceptionally high demand is often not feasible either. Further, in some cases, student veterans are not interested in taking courses that deliberately separate them from their civilian counterparts, because they are seeking opportunities to reintegrate into a nonmilitary community. As one veterans' coordinator explained, "isolating veterans from the rest of the population is not necessarily positive[;] . . . the worst thing we [can] do is continue to isolate them from that immersion and that process" or reinforce "reclusive-veteran stereotypes" (Grasgreen). In other cases, some student veterans choose not to sign up for the veterans-only designated sections because they feel their need or desire to be around other veterans is less acute than it is for some of their "battle buddies," so they don't sign up in order to allow others with a perceived greater need to do so. A concern that veterans-only classes might be stigmatized as "remedial" is another apprehension some veterans voice.

Institutions offering veterans-only courses have recognized that providing professional development opportunities to faculty to ensure clarity of purpose is crucial (see Sura). While the impulse of an instructor to teach a veterans-only course may be well-meaning, doing so without a keen sense of the varied motives for military service, as well as the complexity of the many different kinds of professional work service members have engaged in, can lead to profound assumptions and misconceptions about the students in the class. For instance, notorious cultural divides exist between different branches of the military, and those divides may find their way into the classroom. Army veterans may, for reasons that have nothing to do with collegiate life, dismiss contributions to the course by Navy veterans. Even deeper schisms often exist between ranks, or, perhaps most poignantly, between combat veterans and noncombat veterans (though those lines are increasingly blurry). It is worth noting again that the stereotypical conception of the student veteran experience includes combat. Such visions, as we demonstrated earlier, are contrary to the actualities: many service members will never have been deployed to a foreign country, and among those who have, many will not have served in an active war zone, let alone engaged in direct combat. Certainly, services members working in a military at war will and do feel the effects of those wars—even those working in an office in the Pentagon or a missile silo in Wyoming are immersed in a culture of war—but the figure of the combat-hardened (male)[8] soldier or Marine that occupies a central place in our imaginations has displaced the realities of a very large, complex, and diverse military force (see Chapter 1). Instructors without knowledge of this complexity, or at least sensitivity to it, not only undermine their own credibility, but also jeopardize the possibility of fashioning a safe zone for student veterans that is the very purpose of most veterans-only classes.

Further, we would point out that the governing assumption of most veterans-only classes is that veterans are in need of some sort of buffer from the rest of the student body. Indeed, such classes are predicated on students' deficits, most often characterized by diagnostic medical and psychological language. When courses' starting points are the presumption of need for rehabilitation or, more simply, protection, broader educational goals can be sacrificed. Later, we recommend an asset-based approach that reorients class creation away from an underlying vision of veterans as deficient and toward a vision of veterans as students with notable assets.

VETERAN-FOCUSED COURSES

Some institutions have responded to (or even anticipated) the enrollment challenges and pedagogical hurdles that veterans-only classes pose, and one resulting strategy has been to form courses that take the veteran or the military as their subject without limiting enrollments to veterans. These classes are specifically marketed to service members, their families, or others affected by war, and while enrollment is not limited to those particular students, their presumed interests and anticipated engagement are central motivations for such courses.

Publication of a wide range of teaching materials that engage with issues of war has facilitated the development of these courses. For example, OIF Army infantryman Alex Horton's essay "On Getting By: Advice for College-Bound Vets" has been anthologized in one of Norton's FYW readers, and Jena McGregor's essay "Military Women in Combat" appears in Bedford's bestselling FYW anthology *Current Issues and Enduring Questions,* which also includes a complete section titled "Service: A Duty? A Benefit? Or Both, or Perhaps Neither?" Accordingly, faculty have created syllabi with sequences focused on the wars themselves or some aspect of them. For example, torture became a common topic for student writing after Abu Ghraib, as did the issue of the draft, military recruitment on college campuses, the idea of a "just war," and similar topics.

Course sequences and lessons on these topics, however, are not precisely what we mean by veteran-focused courses. By veteran-focused, we mean those courses whose genesis or revision stem from the attempt to address within a curriculum the needs of veterans, military family members, or others affected by military action. They are courses in which faculty members arrange course materials and activities by focusing on the needs of the veteran population in order to recruit veterans to the course. Veteran-focused courses envision veterans as the primary audience for the course, and the engagement with materials about war functions, in part, to attract students with a particular experience or interest in the military, combat, or the effects of war. The faculty teaching veteran-focused classes may also attempt to address the needs of student veterans by crafting what they regard as especially relevant writing assignments for these students.[9]

The veteran-focused classroom provides a meaningful learning environment for veterans because it rests on a deliberate attempt to understand the values of the student veteran population, and, often, their family members. Those needs may be quite straight-forward. They may include providing students options on writing assignments so that they can choose whether or not to disclose their veteran status, providing students with options on seating within a classroom, providing accommodations for out-of-classroom responsibilities (such as work, Reserve or National Guard duty, medical appointments, or family obligations), or providing options on readings or film viewings for veterans who find particular texts or images difficult to endure.[10] Further, faculty development on how to handle the complexities of the wartime experience helps ensure the classroom remains a safe place for intellectual curiosity. For example, helping faculty negotiate the issue of combat casualties may require extensive support, or, more subtly, helping faculty understand that even seemingly supportive statements such as, "I could never imagine what you've been through" may result, as Phil Klay notes, in the veteran feeling "in a corner by himself, able to proclaim about war but not discuss it" while simultaneously shutting out the civilian "from a conversation about one of the most morally fraught activities our nation engages in—war."[11]

For those considering a veteran-focused course, then, we suggest that it be developed in coordination with other stakeholders in veterans' issues on campus. The image we have of a "veteran" may bear very little resemblance to the actual veterans on a particular campus, so identifying local campus trends in veteran demographics is crucial (see Chapter 1 and Chapter 5). Some campuses, for example, may have primarily Air Force veterans, others primarily Marines. Some campuses may have a veteran population concentrated in an MBA program, whereas on others veterans may be concentrated in undergraduate offerings in international studies, engineering, or social work. Some campuses may have a high concentration of combat veterans, whereas others may have a high concentration of support personnel. Some campuses may have a rich tradition of veterans of foreign militaries on a campus, or they may have an unusually high concentration of female veterans, or a large number of military dependents. Understanding these distinctions and others[12] provides a foundation for crafting intentional courses.

Often, veterans' services offices have demographic information that can be useful, but simply opening discussions within a writing department or program is important to ensure a clear understanding of the student veteran population on campus. In other words, forming a veteran-focused class requires nuanced understanding of the veterans on a campus and in a community. Without such an understanding, the goal of recruiting veterans and their dependents for a class will likely result in some of the same issues that veterans-only courses seem to face: inconsistent enrollments, lack of ability to staff underenrolled classes, and inability to create courses that engage veterans in meaningful ways.

VETERAN-FRIENDLY COURSES

Darren Keast at the City College of San Francisco has written about developing a veteran-friendly writing course, and we would suggest that his model provides an avenue for creating the "safe space" that the veterans-only course attempts to provide while also mitigating the pragmatic problems, such as staff resource allocation and student enrollment, that recur in both veterans-only and veteran-focused courses. By the designation "veteran-friendly," Keast means simply a course that, in its preparation and execution, is mindful of the veteran presence on a campus and in a classroom. It does not limit enrollments, nor does it imply a special focus of the coursework or audience for the class. Instead, the course instructor recognizes the particular strengths and challenges veterans and active-duty service members may bring to a classroom and campus, and those strengths and challenges become a measure by which the instructor organizes class material, activities, and assignments.

Keast's discussion of his course development and accompanying reflection on his process for running the course provide a useful road map for instructors. We would draw attention to two particular aspects of his work. First, Keast envisions his course as mitigating the sense of alienation veterans experience in a university setting while simultaneously providing civilians with "public forums to discuss moral issues related to these wars." Keast emphasizes that a veteran-friendly class provides veterans, as one student reported, with "street cred" in the academic exchange of the class, but that the goals of research and careful argumentation require students to engage with topics beyond personal experience alone. Second, while Keast indicates that his course is "themed," he maintains a focus on his institutional and departmental composition outcomes. The result is that he ultimately sees veterans the same way as he does other students. As he says in the closing of his article: "Veterans and civilian students, from what I can tell from my anecdotal experience with their work, have essentially the same needs as writers." Instead of a veteran-focused class, then, a veteran-friendly class is one whose "primary goal . . . is to create a space broad enough for students with a wide range of experiences and predilections to write essays that engage and challenge them and are informed by careful research." The class, Keast hopes, will "bridge the civilian-military gap that many critics have observed."

Keast's classroom, therefore, is a conscious attempt to bridge a cultural divide within the context of a writing classroom, and it does so by mitigating one of the central concerns of veterans-only classes. That concern is perhaps best articulated by Matt Gallagher, the author of the critically acclaimed Iraq memoir, *Kaboom: Embracing the Suck in a Savage Little War,* and the novel *Youngblood.* In "How to Run a Successful Writing Workshop for Veterans" Gallagher argues that veterans-only writing workshops, for all their promise and good intentions, fail to accomplish one of their primary (often unstated) goals, which is to help veterans more easily join new communities and to ease their transition from the military to civilian life. Gallagher observes that for all the benefits of veterans-only writing workshops, their exclusive nature "reinforce[s] an ugly undercurrent of thought in military writing—that one shouldn't write about war unless one participated in it as a combatant or otherwise survived its destruction." Gallagher argues that for veteran writing workshops to work, "they [need] to stress the writing part over the veteran part," and while his position focuses on creative writing, his final words point to what much of our research identifies as well, which is that "inclusion" should start with a broadminded approach of how "to involve talented, driven people" in giving voice to complex issues.

From our perspective, then, the veteran-friendly class model offers the most viable opportunity for many schools to address veteran enrollments in writing classes. On the one hand, such courses recognize veterans as a group with particular strengths and challenges that recur with some regularity across institutions, and, on the other hand, they provide a means of, to invoke military language, remobilization that allows student veterans more transparency in making their educational decisions. Whereas even a veteran-focused class relies on the notion of "the veteran" to animate the course material (effectively asking veterans to participate in the class as veterans), the veteran-friendly class acknowledges without insisting on the role that the veteran identity may have played in shaping a sense of self while the student negotiates new roles as civilian and student. The classroom becomes a space where both the veteran identity and the student identity can be honored and performed.

With that in mind, here are some general principles to facilitate a veteran-friendly writing classroom:

Principle 1: Include a Syllabus Statement Indicating an Awareness of the Complexities of Being a Student Veteran
Here is an example created by Katt Blackwell-Starnes:

> I recognize the complexities of being a student veteran. If you are a student veteran, please inform me if you need special accommodations. Drill schedules, calls to active duty, complications with GI Bill disbursement, and other unforeseen military and veteran-related developments can complicate your academic life. If you make me aware of a complication, I will do everything I can to assist you or put you in contact with university staff who are trained to assist you. (Hart and Thompson, "An Ethical Obligation")

Principle 2: Follow Keast's Advice and Encourage Veterans to "Contribute Their Own Expertise to Class Discussions"
As Keast notes, "Student veterans often report having their experiences overlooked, undervalued, or unappreciated by civilian soci-

ety," so inviting student veterans to share those experiences and to frame them in language accessible to their civilian classmates can facilitate an inclusive classroom environment.

Chapter 4 Implementation Questions

- Has your institution attempted any of the three types of courses we describe in this chapter?
- If so, has offering it been sustainable? If not, what barriers may have prevented the offerings?
- Does your campus have a large enough student veteran population to allow for long-term investment in veterans-only or veteran-focused curricula?
- Does your course/curriculum allow for flexibility in attendance policies to accommodate a student veteran's potentially complicated schedule?
- What resources does your university/college/community have that you can refer a student veteran to?
- What ground rules do you establish for class discussions, and do they make room for all students to feel as if their personal experiences and perspectives will be honored?

5

Engaging Veteran Trauma

THROUGHOUT THIS STUDY, WE HAVE emphasized that an asset approach to student learning provides the best pathway for understanding the student veteran demographic. The reasons for that focus are simple: our research and the research of others (perhaps most prominently, that published by Chris Cate, vice president for research at Student Veterans of America) has repeatedly demonstrated that veterans, especially in four-year colleges, are highly successful and possess core traits of our strongest students. Indeed, they often are our best students (see "Student Veterans: A Valuable Asset"). Like many from eras past,[1] today's student veterans are persistent, resilient, inquisitive, and, as we discussed earlier, focused on the benefits that higher education affords them as they move into careers in the civilian sector. Nonetheless, a significant number of student veterans using the Post-9/11 GI Bill carry with them war experiences that have few parallels in other students' lives, and indeed, some student veterans will arrive at school enduring both physical and emotional trauma. To close this volume, then, we'd like to address one particular feature of many first-year writing classrooms that can lead to disclosure of trauma: the personal essay.

A wide range of scholarship exists on trauma and the classroom, and while we find in it powerful ruminations on what war trauma may mean for students and faculty, we want again to emphasize that the pathologizing of veterans is as great a concern for faculty as the possibility of teaching a student enduring PTSD, TBI, Military Sexual Violence, or other types of war trauma. The numbers bear this out. According to the National Center for PTSD, "[a]bout 11–20 out of every 100 Veterans (or between 11–20%) who served

in OIF or OEF have PTSD in a given year" ("How Common").
While this is an unprecedented acknowledgment of war trauma,
within any particular cohort of student veterans in a university
class, the percentage negotiating the complex trauma that comes
with war is likely to be even lower (see Vacchi and Berger). Accordingly, our study has focused on the overwhelming benefits of
student veterans on campus, even while we recognize at this point
the need to address a common concern among faculty that appears
in a wide body of scholarship. To do so, we situate the discussion
of trauma around the personal essay because of its wide use across
the country. While some writing programs either prohibit or do
not explicitly encourage personal essays as part of their curriculum,
our research suggests that it remains a mainstay in many college
writing classes.

Within the field of writing studies, debates continue about the
role of personal writing assignments, and much of that debate
centers on the challenges personal disclosure poses for writing instructors. Despite the debates in the field (Williams Mlynarczyk;
Goldblatt), our 2011 survey of writing program administrators and
writing instructors revealed that more than two-thirds of respondents assign personal narrative essays and/or journals or blogs.[2] Additionally, as Janet Lucas points out, even in composition classes
that ostensibly focus on academic writing, "students continue to
disclose themselves." Therefore, as Lucas argues, "the question becomes how to respond thoughtfully, intelligently, and professionally to these disclosures" (368).

Disclosure about war trauma can be especially complicated.
Scholars in trauma studies have identified different types of trauma,
and among them is one that few faculty are equipped to negotiate—perpetrator trauma. When faculty think about trauma, they
often think about the survivors. In terms of student veterans, this
manifests itself in faculty thinking about the ongoing stress service
members are under while in a war zone, the traumatizing effects on
the mind and body of being under fire or actually enduring physical wounds after being shot, or the ongoing trauma of service members who have been injured either directly or indirectly by explosive

devices. They may also consider the only recently acknowledged pervasiveness of Military Sexual Violence. In all of these scenarios, the veteran has been the recipient of violence in some form or fashion. And yet combat veterans have also been the perpetrators of violence, and in that role many experience life-altering emotional and physical trauma.

To be clear, the idea of "perpetrator trauma" is wrought with deeply consequential moral questions, as the word *perpetrator* itself carries with it a connotation of guilt or even active disregard for the well-being of others.[3] In the field of trauma studies, however, the term is meant to be more descriptive than prescriptive; it describes a type of traumatic experience or action more than it prescribes how we should judge or moralize about the nature of that type of trauma. Certainly, some scholars, such as Claude Lanzmann, make strong arguments about the evil of perpetrator violence and the "absolute obscenity" of trying to understand it. Alan Gibbs discusses the fraught history of the term, even suggesting that PTSD as a cultural designator may create psychological constructions that, for Gibbs and others, are hardly objective or reliable (45–49). Still, for scholars like Cathy Caruth (often considered the founder of trauma studies within literary and some social science circles), anyone who endures trauma is by definition a victim, even if also a perpetrator. Indeed, that trait has come to stand as a central piece of what is sometimes called "Caruthian Trauma Theory." Regardless of the debates within that field, it may be useful for scholars in writing studies to think of the term as one that attempts to capture a type of emotional and physical harm that a person actively commits.

The distinction is important because within combat situations, there are instances in which a service member may do harm to someone who is a noncombatant or to structures that should not be the object of attack—personal property, farms, cultural artifacts, or even the landscape. The violence of war often extends far beyond any particular individual's intent in war. As Shannon Meehan and Roger Thompson have demonstrated, even soldiers who mean to do well, who follow all appropriate protocols, and who even go beyond those protocols to ensure the safety of civilians, may still commit a war atrocity, and in doing so, face consequences—both personal and professional, emotional and spiritual—few others can fully appreciate. Such observations do not change the fact that the victims of American service members' actions suffer extraordinary and unimaginable loss, but it also recognizes the fact that the perpetrators return home and seek out new lives, all in the shadow of their past actions. In the case of American universities, faculty with combat veterans in their classes are as likely to have students enduring perpetrator trauma as they are to have students enduring survivor trauma. Indeed, they may have both.

So, how do faculty, especially those who teach personal essays or narratives, or who use journals or reflective writing in their classes, respond ethically to the revelation of war trauma? Certainly, considerable research in WS and in the health professions supports the claim that "when individuals write about emotional experiences, significant physical and mental health improvements follow" (Pennebaker 162). Studies of World War II veterans, in particular, have shown that "the most effective way of dealing with traumatic memory is to develop some kind of story or narrative about the event" and that "veterans who used an active processing strategy, one where they tried to give meaning to the traumatic events of the war, succeeded quite well in taking the trauma out of their traumatic memories" (Hunt and Robbins 62–63). Similarly, studies of Vietnam veterans participating in oral history projects demonstrated that in sharing their stories, "veterans and their student listeners believed they could contribute to the 'healing' and reconciliation that veterans' organizations . . . placed at the top of the nation's post-Vietnam agenda" (Hagopian 594). Veterans from the current wars have also benefited from storytelling. For example, William Isler, chief of clinical health psychology at Lackland (Texas) Air Force Base's mental health facility, has found that "in PTSD treatment, it isn't the avoidance [that helps], it's the retelling, writing it down, adding more descriptors" (R. Wilson et al. 397).

Perhaps even more strikingly, some within the military have called for closer attention to writing as a healing activity—and indeed as an activity to retain soldiers after battle. We include one such example in the Writing/Practices 2. In an op-ed written for *Infantry Magazine*, Captain Daniel Shell argues that the metacognitive processes of writing contribute to a more stable force during and after combat. As a result, he argues for focused writing instruction as part of military training. So, while many writing instructors may ask, as Dan Morgan did in considering his own ethical responsibilities concerning the disclosure of trauma in a first-year composition class, "Is it appropriate for an English teacher to nudge a student toward rethinking the traumas of her life?" (320), we should also be cognizant of the fact that "telling those stories is central to the healing process for [veterans] and for society at large. Soldiers who have experienced trauma and loss should [therefore] be given the opportunity and the space to tell their story, and we should be willing to listen and believe" (Kiely and Swift 358).

Of course, a central question arises: is the writing classroom, especially the first-year writing classroom, the appropriate venue for such storytelling and disclosure? Instead of trying to provide a global response to that question or a final statement for how programs should best approach the issue of war trauma disclosure in writing classrooms—a statement that would inevitably fail to capture the complexity of the issues at stake—we instead provide below some sense of the range of practices across the country. From that range, we will suggest some general guidelines that writing instructors and WPAs may deploy in confronting the challenges posed by classrooms where war trauma surfaces and consider some of the advantages of such public disclosures. While some veterans will want to write about their service experiences and others will not, we as writing faculty nonetheless need to be aware that

> the intimate nature of writing itself serves as both a stimulus and a catharsis for past experiences. When those feelings are expressed, the teacher cannot avoid or dismiss them. To do so would be negligent on our parts. If our role as teachers is to establish an atmosphere of trust in which students can express feelings and attitudes freely without threat of condemnation or personal judgment, we have an ethical and a legal responsibility to effectively respond and refer if necessary. It is not

expected that we must "cure" or solve these problems. (Valentino, "Responding")

We need to be prepared for those disclosures, so that, unlike Melanie Burdick, we do not feel afraid to respond to war stories or wonder "how to critique these writings just the right way, without becoming lost in depression" (354) ourselves.

RESPONSES TO DISCLOSURE

Perhaps the most notable story of war disclosure in a writing classroom comes from the Community College of Baltimore County (CCBC). There, Linda De La Ysla, an experienced writing faculty member, encountered writing by a student veteran that would eventually make national headlines (Walker; "Charles Whittington"). While the event was widely publicized, a succinct retelling will be useful. Charles Whittington was a student veteran in De La Ysla's composition class, and as part of an assignment to compose "narrative essays about a significant event" (De La Ysla 99), he wrote a provocative piece in which he essentially admitted to the thrill that killing can bring with it: "Killing is a drug to me and has been ever since the first time I have killed someone. At first, it was weird and felt wrong, but by the time of the third and fourth killing it feels so natural. It feels like I could do this for the rest of my life and it makes me happy" ("Veteran's Essay"). Whittington later published the piece of writing in the school newspaper, and in short order, was suspended from campus, deemed a threat to the community.

The nature of the disclosure in this instance may seem extreme on several counts. First, it involves writing about a topic that some might consider worthy of censorship. Additionally, it involves writing for multiple audiences, including the faculty member, class peers, and, importantly, the larger campus community. Even further, it involves a degree of honesty about perpetrator violence—during a time of war no less—that unsettled more than a few students, teachers, and administrators, not to mention the public. In all, it was a remarkable moment that may seem an outlier in many respects, even while it provides a moment of clarity into the complexity of the issue of war trauma in the writing classroom.

The point here is not to debate the rightness or wrongness of the student, the writing assignment, the faculty member, the campus newspaper staff, the student body of the school, the administration, or any of their decisions. Instead, the point for the purposes of our study is to help bring into sharp relief the complexity of personal writing, war, trauma, and how they might intersect in the class-room. The example at CCBC illustrates how, when students write about personal matters, they stand not only to gain some sense of healing (per some of the studies mentioned above) or reorientation to their trauma, but also to have that trauma reinscribed and retold by unexpected audiences or participants in a discussion about student veterans' role on campus. When a narrative becomes public, the narrator may have little control over that story. That loss of control is itself troubling, and indeed, may be particularly trouble-some for those already enduring war trauma.

Of course, disclosure within a classroom may lead to the opposite result as well, whereby students gain control over an aspect of their lives that had previously been out of control. For example, a writing instructor at a regional comprehensive in the Midwest shared a story of how, when a student disclosed her role in Abu Ghraib, the student was able to use her own class writing as a vehicle for seeking professional help. It was a piece of writing in response to a class reading about torture, and the student did not expect the writing assignment to lead to discussion about her role in OIF. But, as she composed, she found herself making a case based upon her own experiences. In doing so, she realized the depth of the moral quandaries she continued to struggle with, and, with the help of the instructor, found her way to the school's counseling center.

These stories are brackets—one involving student writing that led to ostracization, the other involving student writing that led to reconciliation—between which linger countless variations, from minor observations about the power of the writing process to fa-cilitate clearer thinking and genuine insight to major interventions to prevent self-harm or harm of others. No attempt to codify such a range would be successful, simply because the permutations are too extensive and, in some cases, too profound to capture with a short study. Still, guidance is warranted,[4] and the principles below represent our guidance for responding to war trauma in the writing classroom, especially as it might emerge in a student veteran's personal writing.

We note again, however, that we introduce these at the end of this book purposefully. It's a rhetorical move to help our readers understand and appreciate the fact that student veteran trauma, while pressing and real, is not the typical story of veterans on college campuses. The most common story is one of success and, indeed, excellent performance. Forgetting that leads to significant barriers to student veteran success on campus. If trauma is the starting point of engagement with student veterans, any initiative to help or facilitate veteran transitions launches on shaky, and indeed misleading grounds.

PRINCIPLES FOR WRITING FACULTY RESPONDING TO WAR TRAUMA

These principles are intended to help faculty establish some of the boundaries within which they might attend to the needs of students enduring war trauma. It's worth noting here that these guidelines are meant to address the needs of veterans' trauma. War trauma, of course, extends beyond just the combatants. Noncombatant victims of war, migrants fleeing armed conflict, asylum seekers, health care and aid workers, family members of others caught in a war zone—a wide range of war trauma may emerge in any writing classroom. This volume's focus, however, is on the student veteran experience, and while some of these guidelines may be transferable to other war trauma, we recommend that faculty who have students negotiating other aspects of such trauma seek experts in those domains.

Principle 1: Personal Narrative Assignments Should Take into Account the Heuristic Possibilities of Narrative in Fostering Disclosure of Trauma

While any type of writing may lead to disclosure of trauma, personal essays and other types of personal or "expressivist" writing are more likely to invite such disclosures. As a result, we recommend that faculty evaluate the benefits of the personal narrative as a classroom artifact within their institution, not just in terms of the rhetorical strategies faculty hope students learn from them or the ways in which personal writing may help students to imagine themselves as writers, but in terms of the types of responses those narratives invite. Assignments that ask students to report on a particularly difficult decision they have faced, or an obstacle they have overcome, or a story they have had difficulty telling—all of these provide fertile ground for powerful invention by students, but they also provide opportunities for especially complicated disclosures.

Of course, some faculty engage with these sorts of writing as part of an intentional process of discovery and critical thinking, and the writing that such prompts elicit can be deeply engaging—for the writers and their audiences. Even so, when veterans populate a classroom, these sorts of assignments can be tantamount to "outing" a veteran and their experience. Even if the response is not about a traumatic event, it is likely to call on personal experiences within that student's military experience, especially because so much of military training is predicated on the idea of overcoming obstacles and remaking oneself. So, on campuses where there are sizable numbers of student veterans, we recommend that the WPA initiate a discussion among faculty and invite either a student veteran campus group or the veterans resource officer to attend.

If a personal narrative is a requirement of an FYW curriculum, we think it is an obligation of the faculty to discuss this requirement with the Veterans Services Office (or equivalent) to discern how they might help student veterans negotiate their responses to the assignment or provide alternatives that meet institutional outcomes but mitigate any impact on those who are war trauma survivors and/or perpetrators. While the idea of a "trigger warning" may spring to mind here, our point is not to encourage such warnings but instead to work within one's college community to understand how best to achieve curricular outcomes without causing dilemmas about how to respond on the part of either the writers or faculty members. In many instances, we suspect there will be little to discuss, but in others, the discussion may reveal significant concerns with a required assignment or sequence. Addressing those concerns at the institutional level (see the subsection of De La Ysla's chapter titled "How 'Good' Came from 'Bad'") emphasizes to students and faculty the interrelated nature of programs and departments. It also demonstrates a focus on student well-being and learning.

Principle 2: Provide Resources for Students

All students can benefit from knowing what resources are available to them. In terms of war trauma, student veterans will typically need specialized resources that faculty are generally unable to provide, not for lack of desire or earnestness, but instead simply because of the nature of the types of training required to help people understand trauma and its impact on their lives. In many instances, a college campus may not itself have appropriate resources to help a student veteran, so we recommend that WPAs on campuses with large numbers of combat veterans contact local veterans services offices for advice and for a list of resources to pass on to faculty in the event of student need. The point here is not to assume that trauma results in troubled students, but instead to equip faculty with information so that they can point veterans who make disclosures to qualified assistance.

Principle 3: Acknowledge Disclosures When They Occur

While faculty's role in helping students with war trauma is perhaps best described as that of a guide or "first responder" (see De La Ysla)—a person who can guide student veterans to important resources to help them—it's important that faculty, when confronted with a piece of writing that discloses trauma, acknowledge not just the writing but the trauma itself. Simple language such as "I appreciate your trusting me with your story," or "I can tell this was an important story for you to share" (rather than "I just can't imagine" [see Klay]), acknowledges the risk the student took in making the disclosure without signaling expertise in counseling. Instead, such responses signal that the reader has not only read the text but has also recognized the gravity of the disclosure and can provide an opportunity to point the student to properly trained resources, if such help is warranted. Such reflective statements also honor the privacy of the student's writing even while acknowledging the difficulty of the student's burden.

Of course, faculty are not the only members of a writing class or writing support staff to read student writing. Peer response is a widespread pedagogical practice, and most college writing centers employ undergraduate and/or graduate student consultants. Consequently, faculty must also be prepared to guide these respondents who may find themselves encountering trauma disclosures in student veterans' texts.

Principle 4: Reconsider Assessment When Disclosure Occurs

If trauma disclosure occurs in a piece of graded writing, faculty are faced with a difficult choice: if the writing is not great, should the teacher give the assignment a less-than-desirable grade, or does the fact of the disclosure make grading secondary? Our recommendation is to not "grade" the writing that discloses war trauma. Indeed, if a faculty member is assigning essays that explicitly elicit or purposely ask students for sensitive disclosures, we recommend not grading those pieces of writing at all—whether or not the student is a veteran. Instead, we suggest using them as a stage of the writing process that leads to a document that is more distanced from the trauma, and to assess the final product rather than the earlier stages of writing.

No matter how earnestly a faculty member explains that a grade reflects the effectiveness and quality of the writing, when disclosure occurs, the student has taken great personal risk to share something and assessing that personal risk as equivalent to any other piece of writing misses an important moment—pedagogically, professionally, and personally. It is, in our estimation, appropriate to acknowledge the risk that student took and then to provide an alternative means of achieving a grade. If a curriculum is designed to allow for such exceptions, students with various other traumas may also benefit. Regardless of the alternative chosen, it is important to recognize that grading an assignment that details disclosure of war trauma may constitute a risk to the well-being of the student.

Principle 5: Share and Report

When traumatic war disclosure occurs in student writing, it often demonstrates a deep sense of trust the student has in the faculty member. That trust requires that the faculty member act in good faith on the student's behalf. At the same time, faculty are part of an institution that has its own professional mandates and regulations. Many schools now have formal reporting obligations, yet even in the absence of those, we recommend when trauma disclosure occurs that the faculty member make either their supervisor or the veterans services personnel on campus aware of the disclosure. We want to be clear that notifying others is a form of support, and that the faculty member need not betray trust by revealing detailed information he or she feels is not necessary to share. Still, we want to emphasize that faculty, in fact, have limited contact with students and often only see them for relatively brief periods of time. As a result, they may not have as full of a picture of the student as a supervisor or veterans services staff member may have. So simply a brief email or conversation to say that the student was sharing personal stories that are particularly profound or that deal with war trauma may be sufficient. One need not betray a student's trust by disclosing details or by directly passing on the student's writing.

Sharing such information does not and should not represent a sense of alarm. It simply signals one's understanding that the student is part of a larger community whose networks of support only benefit from more information. Notification that the student is writing about their war experiences can be helpful to campus staff and to the student themself. Indeed, it also provides a contingency that prompts discussion with campus professionals versed in veterans' issues of how to be more supportive of the student. Notification of disclosure will not seem unusual to most veterans services staff, and their awareness that the student wrote about war experiences can be helpful to them. It need not flag that there is a "problem." Instead, it just helps ensure a network of support is prepared and aware, both of the student's needs and the faculty member's.

In rare instances when trauma disclosure implies or includes statements that indicate harm or potential harm to the student or to others, a faculty member must report it to appropriate campus officials. Reporting must be prompt. Most campuses now have a process for such reporting, and WPAs should ensure faculty—including part-time faculty, TAs, and new hires—are aware of those processes if they are not part of regular institutional training.

Writing faculty are frequently in the position of having to negotiate complex emotional issues that students are facing. Disclosure of war trauma is an especially complicated disclosure, and it puts faculty in a position of having to negotiate their roles of, on the one hand, being trusted advisors who are also in positions of authority and power, while on the other hand being employees who have professional responsibilities over which they do not have control. While we recognize the need for student privacy, and we affirm the importance of student trust in faculty for academic and personal success, we also affirm the need of institutions to have information in order to ensure that support and safety are provided to students and faculty. WPAs can mitigate the complexities of this situation by addressing it with faculty as part of training and collaboratively developing a protocol to follow. Faculty can similarly mitigate the complexities by making clear to students that their sharing of personal information may sometimes require them to report the general nature of that disclosure to others.

DEPATHOLOGIZING THE STUDENT VETERAN

We end this chapter self-consciously concerned that the final guideline above plays into stereotypes of combat veterans that are unsupported by research on veterans in higher education and that can be damaging to student veteran populations on campus. We want to emphasize that disclosure—even of trauma, but certainly of the ambiguities of the wartime experience—rarely warrants concern or aggressive intervention. Student veterans remain one of the highest-achieving and most successful groups on campuses, especially at four-year institutions, so any lingering image of the veteran as a threat or a worrisome figure in any way is simply not supported by the abundance of scholarship.

What we hope we have achieved throughout this volume is an

affirmation of the great value student veterans bring to a campus and the tremendous benefits they bring to a writing classroom. To acknowledge those benefits is not to tip into another stereotype—that of the hero who deserves special consideration. Instead, it is to reorient campus culture to reflect what scholarship continues to demonstrate: that student veterans are in most respects like many other adult students, but that they graduate from four-year institutions at higher rates and with higher GPAs than their comparable cohorts. So, while we see war trauma as a serious and pressing issue, and while we have written about it in various ways in other venues, our goal here is to simply put it in its appropriate place—at the end of the consideration of what student veterans bring to campus. Primarily what they bring is success. And our hope is that some of the observations we have made in this chapter do not undermine readers' impressions of that fact.

Chapter 5 Implementation Questions

- What policies do you or your department have concerning student disclosure of trauma?
- Which campus offices provide student support in a timely manner?
- What alternatives to grading an assignment that has prompted disclosure can you develop to ensure both that the student receives writing guidance and that others in the class are treated equitably if an exception is made for the disclosing student?
- What is your or your department's policy when trauma disclosure occurs publicly in a classroom, either through classroom discussion or in peer-review exercises?
- What are your department's or your institution's reporting requirements and what are your legal obligations to report? What protocols do you have in place for addressing the complexities of student disclosure of trauma or other personal information that indicates a potential need for support?

Writing/Practices 2

Pedagogy and Programs

WRITING INSTRUCTION INFLUENCED BY MILITARY EXPERIENCE, VALUES, AND NEEDS

THIS SECTION CONTAINS EXAMPLES OF program and curricular development that occurs within the military or that has been considered within a university to demonstrate how different contexts for instruction inform those decisions. We include a syllabus for a graduate writing course at the Marine Corps University, an article from *Infantry Magazine,* a graduate student veteran's teaching philosophy, and a set of heuristics that we developed for college writing instructors.

The aim of this section is, on the one hand, to illustrate the complexity of course considerations within the military even as, on the other hand, universities shape their own curricula to account for student veterans. We note that among the following examples, readers will find an emphasis on the value of writing as well as the value of considering what one popular textbook for writing classes called "current issues and enduring questions" (Barnet and Bedau). We hope these examples demonstrate the considerable, and likely surprising, overlap between military and university educational cultures.

Example 1

Marine Corps Writing Syllabus
The syllabus that follows was created for a graduate course at Marine Corps University. Officers within the military advance their career by taking courses from a variety of institutions, including accredited uni-

versities housed within service branches. The following syllabus comes from a Marine Corps course and includes readings from a range of both canonical and noncanonical philosophers, politicians, and literary writers that are organized around themes valued within Marine Corps culture. A discussion-based course, its instructor, Major Tim Riemann, took particular pride in the seminar format and its emphasis on discussion around complex ethical issues Marines face as they progress through their careers.

Marine Corps University / Command and Staff College
The Electives Program

Lesson Title: Where Good Ideas Come From   **Date: 4 Jan – 1 Feb 19**
                                                    Author: Maj Timothy Riemann

"PME has stagnated, focused more on the accomplishment of mandatory credit at the expense of lethality and ingenuity."
– Sec Mattis, 2018 National Defense Strategy

1. Introduction
   This course is a reading intensive elective where a student is provided the opportunity to create their own reading syllabus given very broad general categories of study. Each class will have a different theme (ie. "leadership", or "science") and students will be given the latitude to choose the reading material associated with the given topic based on their own interest. The topics are purposely not of a specific military nature, thereby broadening the student's exposure to new ideas, concepts, and ways of thinking.

   Each student will have chosen different material relating to the given topic and the classroom setting will focus on the student presenting a 10-15 minute overview, Q&A, guided discussion, and/or practical application showcasing and exposing the larger class to what they learned. Allowing each student to decide their own reading material and then convening in class to present what they have learned has three tangible benefits: a maximum exposure to new ideas, places the officer in the role of both student and teacher, and offers the best chance for the officers to make new and novel connections of ideas. Students will submit their self-generated syllabus to the instructors for consideration and approval no later than 18 December 2018.

2. Student Learning Outcomes
   1.1 Comprehend a breadth of new material not usually discussed or explored in traditional professional military education curriculum.
   1.2 Explore new and unique ways of condensing and presenting information in a time constrained environment.
   1.3 Understand and develop new and novel connections between divergent and seemingly unrelated pieces of information

3. Supporting Educational Objectives.
   a. Comprehend the roles that factors such as geopolitics, geostrategy, society, region, culture, and religion play in shaping planning and execution of joint force operations across the range of military operations, to include traditional and irregular warfare. [JPME 4f]
   b. Comprehend the role of the Profession of Arms in the contemporary environment. [JPME 6a]
   c. Comprehend the ethical dimension of operational leadership and the challenges that it may present when considering the Profession of Arms. [JPME 6c]
   d. Communicate with clarity and precision. [JMPE 6e]
   e. Analyze the importance of adaption and innovation on military planning and operations. [JMPE 6f]

1

Marine Corps University / Command and Staff College
The Electives Program

4. Student Requirements / Schedule

a. Class 1, 4 January 2019, *Topic: Innovation*

(1) Requirements:

(a) 1300-1400

<u>1</u>. Each student will give a 5 minute introduction about themselves and then participate in a team building exercise lead by the instructors.

<u>2</u>. Students and instructors will review course expectations and requirements.

<u>3</u>. Students will arrive at class having read no less than 200 pages on the topic of innovation. Each student will have prepared a 10-15 minute overview / presentation that covers what they read.

(b) 1400-1500

<u>1</u>. MajGen Mullen, CG TECOM, will come and give an hour long PME on reading. In the event that he is unable to attend, students will continue with their innovation presentation.

b. Class 2, 8 January 2019, *Topic: Leadership*

(1) Requirements: Students will come to class having read no less than 200 pages relating to the topic of leadership. Students will have prepared a 10-15 minute presentation, conversation, and/or Q&A session highlighting and explaining what they read from their reading. Students are encouraged to explore unique ways of presenting information to the class.

(2) Location: Classroom

c. Class 3, 10 January 2018, *Topic: Ethics/Philosophy*

(1) Requirements: Students will come to class having read no less than 200 pages relating to the topic of ethics/philosophy. Students will have prepared a 10-15 minute presentation, conversation, and/or Q&A session highlighting and explaining what they read from their reading. Students are encouraged to explore unique ways of presenting information to the class.

(2) Location: TBD

d. Class 4, 14 January 2019, *Topic: Contemporary Issues*

(1) Requirements: Students will come to class having read no less than 200 pages relating to any contemporary issue of their choice (global warming, education, immigration, health care, etc...). Students will have prepared a 10-15 minute presentation, conversation, and/or Q&A session highlighting and explaining what they read from their reading. Students are encouraged to explore unique ways of presenting information to the class.

(2) Location: TBD

e. Class 5, 16 January 2019, *Topic: Science*

(1) Requirements: Students will come to class having read no less than 200 pages relating to any field of scientific study (biology, cosmology, chemistry, particle physics, etc...). Students will have prepared a 10-15 minute presentation, conversation, and/or Q&A session highlighting and explaining what they read from their reading. Students are encouraged to explore unique ways of presenting information to the class.

2

Marine Corps University / Command and Staff College
The Electives Program

(2) Location: TBD

f. Class 6, 22 January 2019, *Topic: Art*
(1) Requirements: Students will come to class having read no less than 200 pages relating to art. Students will have prepared a 10-15 minute presentation, conversation, and/or Q&A session highlighting and explaining what they read from their reading. Students are encouraged to explore unique ways of presenting information to the class.
(2) Location: TBD

g. Class 7, 24 January 2019, *Topic: The Mind*
(1) Requirements: Students will come to class having read no less than 200 pages relating to the mind (consciousness, psychology, decision making, creativity, neuroscience, etc…). Students will have prepared a 10-15 minute presentation, conversation, and/or Q&A session highlighting and explaining what they read from their reading. Students are encouraged to explore unique ways of presenting information to the class.
(2) Location: TBD

h. Class 8, 28 January 2019, *Topic: Fiction/Poetry*
(1) Requirements: Students will come to class having read no less than 200 pages from a work of fiction or poetry of their choice. Students will have prepared a 10-15 minute presentation, conversation, and/or Q&A session highlighting and explaining what they read from their reading. Students are encouraged to explore unique ways of presenting information to the class.
(2) Location: TBD

i. Class 9, 30 January 2019, *Topic: The Future*
(1) Requirements: Students will come to class having read no less than 200 pages relating to the topic of the future. Students will have prepared a 10-15 minute presentation, conversation, and/or Q&A session highlighting and explaining what they read from their reading. Students are encouraged to explore unique ways of presenting information to the class.
(2) Location: The Krulak Center

j. Class 10, 1 February 2019, *Topic: Free Pic*
(1) Requirements: Students will come to class having read no less than 200 pages relating to any topic of their choice though they will be encourage to read something that someone else presented earlier in the course. Students will have prepared a 10-15 minute presentation, conversation, and/or Q&A session highlighting and explaining what they read from their reading. Students are encouraged to explore unique ways of presenting information to the class.
(2) Location: TBD

5. Assessment
(a) <u>Seminar Presentations (40%)</u> – Each week, students will give a 10-15 minute presentation highlighting, summarizing, and explaining the works / books they read.

3

Marine Corps University / Command and Staff College
The Electives Program

They will then have 10 minutes to answer questions and provide amplifying information based on other students' feedback / comments.

(b) <u>Seminar Participation (40%)</u> – Students will be evaluated on their worthwhile contributions to the weekly discussion. They will be graded not just on the frequency of their comments, but also their ability to make connections between the works presented and their own ideas.

(c) <u>Commonplace Notebook (10%)</u> – Students will be required to keep a handwritten commonplace notebook. This notebook will be reviewed periodically by the instructor. Exact format and content of the commonplace notebook will be determined by the student.

(d) <u>Course Paper (10%)</u> – students will prepare one 2-3 page paper at the end of the course discussing a potential innovative solution to a contemporary military problem or situation.

Lesson Hours:

Lecture	Guest Lecturer	Seminar discussion	Film	Practical Application	Staff Ride/ Battle study	Evaluation/Test	Student Preparation Time	TOTAL HOURS
		20					40	60

Submitted by: Reviewed and Approved:

_____   _____

MATTHEW FLYNN, PH.D.   JONATHAN F. PHILLIPS, PH.D.
ELECTIVES COORDINATOR   DEAN OF ACADEMICS

"I have reviewed this material and it is in conformance with MCU Policy Letter 04-06, use of copyrighted material."

_____   _____

LYNN TESSER, PH.D.   DATE
COPYRIGHT CONTROL MANAGER

4

Example 2

Military Officer's Philosophy of Writing

The following work comes from Infantry Magazine *and reflects the author's knowledge of recent scholarship on writing and trauma. He argues that systematic writing instruction within the Army could aid in readiness by helping soldiers understand service trauma. He further argues that writing instruction should be a central part of military training.*

PROFESSIONAL FORUM

Focused Writing Can Improve Readiness, Retention

CPT DANIEL SHELL

The Army faces a recruiting, readiness, and retention problem. Modernity has brought wondrous technology and products, but these have caused unforeseen negative consequences. Smart phones, social media, highly-processed foods, climate-controlled environments, and online shopping allow people to live more comfortably. Increased comfort, however, has failed to increase contentment and meaning, and mental and physical health have dropped in the United States and much of the developed world.[ ] This crisis brings increased rates of obesity, diabetes, depression, and many other modern maladies. A growing number of Americans cannot meet the standards for enlistment, Soldiers may have issues arise during their service that prevent them from deploying and contributing to accomplishing the nation's missions, and ultimately, many Soldiers leave the service because they cannot meet medical, physical, or psychological standards.[ ] The Army has developed various strategies to combat these issues, but a tool backed by psychological research remains unused. Goal-focused and trauma-focused writing offer an untapped well that the Army could use to combat these growing problems. Individual leaders and the Army should implement a program of goal-focused writing to increase Soldiers' performance and health- and trauma-focused writing to help Soldiers deal with past issues.

Army Chief of Staff GEN Mark A. Milley has declared readiness his number one priority.[ ] Readiness, of course, encompasses many facets of being a Soldier — physical fitness, mental health, dental health, family resiliency, training readiness — and the Army has adopted different means of ensuring Soldiers maintain readiness across various attributes. The Army has addressed these problems through a combination of reactive solutions — ensuring the availability of mental health professionals, offering physical therapy to help Soldiers rehabilitate injuries, and offering military family life counselors for couples and families in need of counseling — and proactive solutions such as increasingly realizing and publicizing the importance of sleep and stress reduction, providing healthier food options in dining facilities, and changing the physical fitness system to reflect more recent knowledge of performance, recovery, and injury reduction. These efforts have improved Soldiers' abilities to prevent and react to problems that may arise. Another tool exists, however, in guided writing to process the past and prepare for the future.

Many psychological empirical studies have demonstrated the effectiveness of writing to process past experiences,

evaluate one's character, or develop and implement goals. The benefits of writing and goal-setting include better performance at work or school and better mental and physical health.[ ] Additionally, developing one's own goals as opposed to being given goals from a leader or organization leads to improved results. One study found that even when students developed goals unrelated to school, their performance on tests improved.[ ] This research suggests that even if Soldiers developed personal goals for pursuits outside the Army, their performance in the Army would likely still improve. Overall, this research suggests goal-focused writing could lead to improved health and performance in Soldiers and thus increased readiness throughout the force.

Writing about experienced trauma has produced similarly positive results. Similar to discussing issues with a social worker, psychologist, or trusted friend, writing about traumatic experiences allows the Soldier to make sense of the trauma. It allows the Soldier to glean the potential wisdom from such experiences and develop a coherent narrative for the event. Different studies have demonstrated significant improvements in people's lives who complete such writing, including the following benefits: "These improvements included fewer consultations with physicians, greater long-term psychological health, and improved immune function."[ ] Though such writing cannot and will not replace counseling, it may reduce the need for some people and aid the counselor, as the Soldier will have already worked on his or her feelings through writing about experiences.

The Army could develop its own writing program to achieve this or use one that already exists. One such program is the Self Authoring Suite, which offers three different guided-writing programs. Future Authoring focuses on developing goals and plans to achieve those goals, Present Authoring helps identify one's virtues or flaws and addresses both, and Past Authoring lets the author develop a narrative about one's life, including traumatic events, to process those experiences.

This goal-setting program has some distinct advantages over some of the others I've seen. First, it is a systematic process with well-thought out prompts and questions, and each piece builds on itself. Second, the positive — but especially the negative — visualization can help motivate Soldiers to pursue their goals. Part of the exercise involves thinking about what will happen if Soldiers achieve their goals, which is helpful, but the truly impactful aspect is visualizing what will happen if they fail and allow their worst habits and tendencies to continue unabated. Soldiers complete this segment before they develop their goals and plan to implement them. This provides a concrete, tangible reason to be motivated to improve, which increases the exercise's effectiveness. Plenty of people have bad habits they want to end or good habits they want to develop, but too many people quit when the initial excitement disappears. Relatedly, many Soldiers perform well at work, but one event may push a Soldier over the edge and cause him or her to spiral downward and suddenly become a poor performer. This exercise can help move the Soldier in the right direction toward self-improvement, ultimately improving the Soldier's resiliency, which contributes to the unit's readiness.

A writing program could be implemented in a number of ways, but offering a goal-focused writing exercise at critical times in Soldiers' careers makes sense. Enlisted Soldiers could complete it at Basic Combat Training or Advanced Individual Training and at every NCO Education System course. Officers could complete it upon beginning the U.S. Military Academy or ROTC and during each officer education system course in their career progression. Because the exercise involves looking out three to five years, Soldiers would return to the exercise at various times throughout their career, and depending on how it is implemented, the Soldiers could return to the program on their own through a website.

Another beneficial time for Soldiers to complete goal-focused writing would be while they complete the Soldier for Life-Transition Assistance Program (SFL-TAP). This would allow them the opportunity to sit down and think how they want to begin the next phase of their lives, not just in terms of getting a job or going to school, but really think about their goals and what will happen, most importantly, if they fail to achieve their goals and let their worst habits and tendencies rule the course of their lives. Many people look forward to exiting the Army but fail to develop their own mission or purpose and mindlessly enter school or find a job. This exercise could help.

Trauma-focused writing could be used for Soldiers seeking behavioral health treatment and, potentially, could be offered to Soldiers if they feel they could use some sorting out but are not pursuing the Army's behavioral health system. This would allow Soldiers to process their issues before seeing a mental health profession and, as research has shown, potentially decrease the need to see mental health professionals. It would not, of course, replace the behavioral health system, but supplement it and allow Soldiers to address problems on their own, just as they might lift weights to address a strength deficiency.

Computers, money, and time would be the biggest hurdles to implementing a focused-writing program. If computers are a limiting factor, then the Army could provide print outs and provide space for Soldiers to write their responses by hand. The benefit to using a computer, of course, is that Soldiers can return to a digital copy of what they wrote and modify it if they so desire from anywhere they have access to the internet.

If using a commercial program, cost may also be an issue. However, one could argue this may cost less than medication or counseling. The programs may both prevent and help treat issues, so these benefits may also offset the cost.

Time would also be an issue to implementing such a program. Time is precious in Army schools, and something would probably have to be cut to make time for a focused-writing program. Instead of a class on SMART (specific, measurable, achievable, relevant, and timely) goals, Army Values, leadership, or a speech from senior leaders, Soldiers could develop goals of their own. This certainly seems to fall under the broader concept of mission command. This also shows Soldiers and leaders a certain amount of respect. Too often Soldiers get lectured, briefed, and trained to try to change behavior. How about we give the Soldiers some responsibility? This would benefit them and the Army. It would reinforce the Army Values, and probable benefits such as increased performance and improved health would likely offset its cost.

Though I hope the Army adopts a focused-writing program, I understand changes at the Army level happen slowly, and the Army does not want to invest in something without knowing it provides cost-effective benefits. For now, junior leaders could easily implement a program in their units across the force. Measures such as Army Physical Fitness Test scores, percentage of Soldiers on profile, sick call use, reenlistment rate, and behavioral incidents could be assessed before and after the use of the goal-focused writing program. These small experiments could provide evidence of the program's effectiveness in increasing readiness and retention. These leaders can then share the results in venues such as this and up the chain of command. My ultimate hope is that if this proves useful, the Army as a whole will adopt such a system.

Notes

[1] Edmund S. Higgins, "Is Mental Health Declining in the U.S.?" Scientific American, 1 January 2017, https://www.scientificamerican.com/article/is-mental-health-declining-in-the-u-s/.

[2] Nolan Feeney, "Pentagon: 7 in 10 Youths Would Fail to Qualify for Military Service," Time, 29 June 2014, http://time.com/2938158/youth-fail-to-qualify-military-service/.

[3] C. Todd Lopez, "Army Chief of Staff Urges Soldiers to Take Responsibility for Unit, Individual Readiness," Army.mil, 11 October 2017, https://www.army.mil/article/195130/army_chief_of_staff_urges_soldiers_to_take_responsibility_for_unit_individual_readiness.

[4] Jordan Peterson and Raymond Mar, "The Benefits of Writing," Selfauthoring.com, https://www.selfauthoring.com/doc/WritingBenefits.pdf.

[5] Ibid.

[6] Ibid.

CPT Daniel Shell was commissioned as an Infantry officer through Ohio State University's Army ROTC in June 2011 after graduating with bachelor's degrees in History and Political Science. After completing the Infantry Basic Officer Leader's Course and Ranger School, he served in the 1st Battalion, 32nd Infantry Regiment in 3rd and 1st Brigade, 10th Mountain Division. During this time he deployed to Afghanistan and served as a rifle platoon leader, rifle company executive officer, and assistant operations officer. CPT Shell currently serves in the 2nd Armored Brigade Combat Team, 1st Infantry Division.

Example 3

Student Veteran Teacher's Philosophy of Education
Anthony (Tony) Albright served in the US Army, 1st Special Forces Group, from 2001 to 2005. Tony holds an MA in theatre arts from the University of North Dakota, a BA in theatre arts from the University of Minnesota, Morris, and an AA in humanities from Centralia College and is currently pursuing a PhD in rhetoric, writing, and culture at North Dakota State University, where he also serves as a graduate instructor.

Albright's philosophy of teaching (included below), though couched in terms of "duty," clearly belies the simplistic vision of military veterans as holding views about the purpose of education that are antithetical to critical thinking and critique, not to mention creativity. Our aim in including it is to emphasize the ways that a culture of student-centered education can be grounded on the military experience, and within the writing you will see terms like obstacles, strategies, *and* structure *that resonate with both military and university audiences. You can see more of Albright's writing and his reflections on his service by visiting his blog:* https://anthonyjalbright.wordpress.com/.

My goal for the future of my students is to broaden the way they approach their world. I want to influence the way they think, and ensure that they are comfortable overcoming any obstacle encompassing the scope of their lives. Overall, a constructivist approach to doing this seems best. I will allow my students to make their own mistakes and solve their own problems with me as a guide and facilitator. They will learn ways of solving problems that work for them. They will carry that knowledge over to the next problem they face, and the next. If they learn to approach and tackle challenges in this way, to take something from each experience, my teaching will continue to benefit them for the rest of their lives and continue to help me grow as they teach me new ways of solving problems.

I believe in an eclectic approach to education, in contrast to the many attempts to place education into a mold that will fit every student. This simply is not plausible. We are all unique people who learn in a diverse range of ways. No one strategy, no matter how good, or how much time was spent developing it, will work for every student. A combination of social reconstruction, progressivism, and existentialism is what I have found most helpful. The order and qualities of these would depend, not just on the student, but on the socioeconomic environment and specific makeup of my class.

Students need to understand and have strategies to deal with the problems they will face when they enter the world beyond school. Students need to be exposed to the kind of group work and social experiences that progressivism prescribes and that they will encounter in social situations for the rest of their lives. It is of fundamental importance that students come away from school with an understanding of how social interactions and group dynamics will affect their professional lives. I believe that my students should be taught to be free-thinking. They should learn to engage in a critical conversation with the authors of the books they read, the news they hear, and even those giving them lectures. They need to understand that knowledge creation comes from discourse, not by rote. None of these philosophies, however, can stand alone as a standard for all students; teachers need to engage in hybrid creation based upon their students' needs. This is an ongoing cycle, not something that can be created and then stored. The teacher informs the student, who informs the teacher, who informs the student. The cycle has no end.

Students learn best when certain conditions are met. They must be interested in and actively engaged in what they are learning. This is the responsibility of the teacher and will require adjustment, improvisation, and a keen perception of the needs of individual students. Students must be taught to work successfully with others to accomplish difficult goals. They must be taught to depend on one another and to see the importance of building and maintaining the relationships that lead to a successful project, and they must, at times, learn what an unsuccessful collaboration looks like as well. The classroom should not be comfortable. It should be a place where students are challenged and held accountable for complacency. It is the teacher's responsibility to make the content interesting and keep their students on task. Teachers who fail to do these things fail their students and do not foster the opportunities for optimum learning that this environment would provide.

Education must have purpose. It must have underlying themes that underpin the entire curriculum. These themes must include a desire to encourage students to develop creative ways of thinking, to provide students with the base of common knowledge necessary for life as a member of an informed electorate, and to prepare students for the various careers and trades that they are actively pursuing. Students must think creatively in order to overcome obstacles that they have never before faced. If they have this basis on which to act, they will never become lost. The classroom should be a place where a student can begin to decide what the rest of life should accomplish. The better prepared students are to make that choice, the better job we have done as teachers.

We must always endeavor to instill in our students a desire to think and act independently of expectations, traditions, and norms. We must teach them to understand a structure, but not to be ruled by it. If we teach them to think creatively, and to quest after knowledge, we will have taught them all they need to know to create new knowledge. We must remember that not everyone will learn the same way. We must use this knowledge to reach as many of our students as possible, through every means necessary. It is our duty and privilege as teachers to empower the free thinkers of the future. Let us not now shirk our duties.

Example 4
Heuristics for WPAs and Writing Faculty Working with Veteran Populations

In the following section, we provide a set of questions that we hope can help shape an institution's response to a significant influx of veterans. We intend these questions as a kind of tear sheet primarily for WPAs or writing faculty, even though we think most are applicable across disciplinary lines. The goal is to help faculty initiate a discussion about veterans in their classroom and to provide a way to gather an initial set of data with which faculty can work. As we have indicated elsewhere in this volume, once an investigation has been made, it may be that a systemic response is not warranted. Our hope, however, is that the decision whether to respond or not is grounded in the types of data that these questions will elicit.

In other places, we have argued that pursuit of "best practices" in veterans studies is neither possible nor desirable.[1] Indeed, Thompson has argued that such a move is unethical on a number of fronts and functions as a type of arhetorical institutional violence. Instead of providing such a list, therefore, we offer here a set of questions that we recommend campus and program leaders consider in order to generate responses to their local student veteran populations as these students go through the process of transitioning from military service to higher education and life as civilians. These questions are intended as starting points, and should not be seen as restrictive and final, but as generative and initial.

Question 1: What is the size of the veteran population on your campus and how many student veterans enroll in FYW or other writing classes on your campus?

Veteran populations on campuses vary widely, even if the vast majority of student veterans are undergraduates (Queen, Lewis, and Ralph). Community colleges have seen the most significant veteran enrollments (see Chapter 3), as large numbers of student veterans begin their higher education at the two-year college level. Online universities also have seen significant veteran and military enrollments.[2] Often, on college campuses that are within close proximity to large military bases,[3] the size of the military-affiliated student population is well known and a subject of institutional discussions and negotiations. Many others have begun such discussions as well. A 2012 study of 690 institutions of higher education conducted by the American Council on Education (ACE) found that "[m]ore than half of all responding institutions . . . provide programs and services specifically designed for military service members and veterans, and approximately 71 percent . . . indicated that providing programs and services for military service members and veterans is a part of their long-term strategic plan" (McBain et al. 7). However, some institutions likely have yet to fully appreciate the size of the veteran population on their campuses. Without knowing those numbers and without understanding precisely what path student veterans typically take when enrolling in writing classes, formulating a response (if needed) is virtually impossible. As we noted earlier, student veterans may take many pathways to FYW classes, but making contact with a veterans resource officer (described below) is a good initial step to help WPAs initiate an inquiry into these numbers.

Question 2: What branches of the military are the primary sources of the student veterans on your campus?

Veteran enrollments vary by region, and regional variations often reveal underlying differences in the types of veterans that enroll on a campus. While the Army remains the largest military branch, veterans from the Air Force, Navy, Marines, and Coast Guard are all eligible for military educational benefits such as the GI Bill and are increasingly finding their way onto college campuses.[4] Some campuses will have no noticeable pattern of enrollments, but others will have distinct patterns of enrollments, perhaps with a primary group from one branch at one point and another branch in a subsequent year. Understanding those variations can help faculty not just to take into account the general backgrounds of student veterans, but also to develop some sense of the genres of writing their students are likely to have composed while serving.

Question 3: Is your campus primarily enrolling veterans from the officer or the enlisted ranks?

While there may be occasional exceptions, in general, military officers have already received an undergraduate degree, whereas enlisted service members typically join the military with only a high school diploma. Most undergraduate student veterans, then, tend to be enlisted,[5] though, again, your campus may be an exception. Inasmuch as many student veterans have spent at least four years in the service, they often resemble other adult learner populations who, though having graduated from high school, have experienced a significant gap in time since attending a civilian academic institution (Navarre Cleary and Wozniak). Yet, unlike many of their civilian counterparts, nearly one-third of post-9/11 "nontraditional" student veterans have taken college courses while serving on active duty ("I Am" 2), and many will have military-issued Joint Service Transcripts containing transfer credits based on their professional education and training. As Jennifer Steele, Nicholas Salcedo, and James Coley explain,

> [T]he ability to obtain academic credit for coursework and training received in the military is important to many veterans. Because student veterans tend to be older than other undergraduates, their persistence in higher education often depends on their ability to make rapid progress and build on the knowledge they established in the military. (30)

WPAs, therefore, may want to familiarize themselves with the American Council on Education (ACE) *Guide to the Evaluation of Educational Experiences in the Armed Services* in order to be prepared to evaluate the feasibility of authorizing credit for the military equivalent of civilian writing courses *(Military Guide)*. For example, an Army veteran who has successfully completed the Basic Public Affairs Specialist–Writer course at the Defense Information School at Fort Meade may be eligible to receive "3 semester hours in news writing" in "the lower-division baccalaureate/associate degree category," while a Navy veteran who has successfully completed the Advanced Communication Manager course at the Fleet Training Center in San Diego may be eligible to receive "2 semester hours in technical writing." In other words, many service members may already have taken college or college-equivalent writing courses, and understanding the nature of those experiences will be crucial in responding to their needs on your campus.

Question 4: Are there any patterns to the MOS designations of veterans on your campus?

MOS stands for Military Occupation Specialty, and it reflects the extensive training a student veteran received in the military to become an expert in the field to which they were assigned. Often, their assignment to a type of military occupation is linked to their performance on a set of examinations. MOSs can vary significantly, from culinary specialist to electronics technician, and different service branches have varying terminology. Nonetheless, across branches all MOSs are bound by the idea that an individual engages in extensive training to become a specialist in a particular field. Even in the Marine Corps, where every Marine is first trained to be a rifleman, the MOSs range from ammunition to signals intelligence. To be selected for an MOS requires hands-on, in-the-field training as well as coursework and various types of examinations, many of them written. The examinations are high stakes in that they are linked to advancement in that occupational field and promotion to higher rank.

For faculty, patterns of MOSs on a campus can provide useful understandings of the types of student veterans one is likely to encounter in the classroom. For example, because certain MOSs are primarily bureaucratic, knowing an MOS can help determine whether a student veteran will readily consider the feasibility of transferring their professional writing experiences to academic writing. Further, it can help determine the likelihood that a student veteran might have either been deployed to a combat zone or been part of combat action. A Marine infantry specialist deployed during OIF or OEF, for example, is far more likely to have experienced combat than an Air Force missile and space systems maintenance specialist in service during the same time frame. Still, assumptions about a student veteran or groups of student veterans based on MOSs should be examined, as the nature of a particular MOS may change over time, and, as Sherry Shi's Veterans Day speech (included in Writing/Practices 1 earlier in this volume) makes clear, not all duties assigned to military personnel are related to their MOSs. Faculty should also refrain from assuming that student veterans will choose a major or field of study related to their MOS. In fact, according to the 2016 SVA survey, 62.5 percent of student veteran respondents claimed their major was "not similar at all" to their MOS, while fewer than 10 percent described their major as "very similar" or "exactly the same" as their MOS (Cate and Davis).

Question 5: What services does your campus provide for veterans?

An estimated 62 percent of US higher education institutions currently provide programs and services designed to serve active-duty military service members and/or student veterans (McBain et al). According to Alexander Taylor, Rodney Parks, and Ashley Edwards, "public universities are the most likely of all institutional types to have a designated veterans' services office. This is largely because GI Bill recipients receive education benefits calibrated to in-state tuition, so most of them attend public institutions" (52). If your institution has a Veterans Service Office (VSO) or veterans affairs office, connecting with their personnel can provide opportunities to identify student veterans and to assist them as they negotiate their college experience.

Even if a separate VSO does not exist on your campus, it is important to know about some key personnel who typically populate those offices. The first is an institution's Certifying Official. The Certifying Official is an on-campus specialist who has been extensively trained to ensure that eligible students receive their federal and state (if applicable) military education benefits ("Role"). The Certifying Official will usher student veterans through the complexities of military benefits, and they certify that specific courses are allowable under GI Bill or other benefits criteria. The Certifying Official is also often a key ally in advising student veterans. Many well-meaning faculty unwittingly guide student veterans to courses or programs that are, in fact, not covered by GI Bill benefits (such as "remedial" or "developmental" writing courses that do not count toward graduation credit). So interaction between a WPA and the Certifying Official at an institution with a high percentage of veterans is crucial to ensure student veteran success. Often, the Certifying Official is a member of the registrar's or financial aid staff, and there may be more than one Certifying Official on campus. On the other hand, at multicampus institutions there might be only one Certifying Official for all campuses.

Besides the Certifying Official, many campuses also now have a veterans resource officer (VRO) or veterans affairs director. In many cases, the veterans resource officer also serves as a Certifying Official, but this is not always the case. The VRO typically coordinates veterans' activities on campus and oversees the general welfare of student veterans. If there is a student veterans' club or Student Veterans of America (SVA) chapter on campus,[6] the VRO typically helps manage the group and ensures they are adequately funded and supported. They often serve as confidants to veterans and service members, as well, are typically housed within student affairs offices, and report to student affairs deans or similar such bodies on a campus. Many, though certainly not all, are themselves veterans, and in recent years, as universities have sought out larger veteran enrollments, the number of VROs has swelled. On many campuses, the VRO will know most of the veterans on campus (including those who are not using GI Bill benefits) and will track data on enrollments and academic success. They also often serve as unofficial academic advisors for many veterans.

As Corey Rumann and Florence Hamrick explain, in addition to appointing a VRO, "[a] second common recommendation is for campuses to designate a private or semi-private campus space as a veterans' lounge where students can gather informally and student veterans' organizations can provide programming, including peer outreach and support" (3). If your institution has a veterans' lounge, this may be a space in which to do some outreach regarding writing support for student veterans. As Marilyn Valentino discovered,

> many student veterans may be reluctant to seek help at the Writing Center, which is outside their 'chain of command.' They'd rather go to their professor. They also may feel that others need tutoring more, the same mindset of sacrificing in battle: when wounded, to check others first. ("Serving" 174)

However,

> [e]xisting veterans' resource centers provide one opportunity to bring the writing center to veterans as a way to meet student-veterans in a place in which many of them already feel more comfortable. . . . [P]lacing a writing consultant within

the veterans' center on a drop-in or walk-in basis improves visibility of writing center services for veterans. (Hinton, "Front and Center" 273)

In other words, if WPAs reach out to collaborate with VROs and/or student veterans' organization leaders (who may alternatively be the ones responsible for the veterans' space on campus), they can build trust while also providing meaningful support to student veteran writers. If student veterans find value in the peer consultations that take place in the veterans' lounge, they not only are more likely to seek help in an existing writing center on campus, but are also more likely to become advocates who encourage other veterans to use the resource to receive feedback on their writing.

Another option, whether or not a veterans' lounge exists on campus, is for the WPA and/or writing center director to recruit student veterans as peer writing consultants. While student veterans may be wary of approaching a civilian "peer"—especially one who may be significantly younger than they are—for feedback on their writing (see Hinton, "Front and Center"), adding student veteran consultants to a writing center staff can be another way of increasing the likelihood that student veterans will take advantage of the resource. For example, when Nancy Effinger Wilson and Micah Wright[7] saw a "disconnect between what [their] writing center was doing and what [they] could/should be doing for [their] student veterans," they created a veterans-tutoring-veterans program "that [they] named the Writing Center Tutor Corps" (2). In doing so, they not only demonstrated to other student veterans that they valued "the unique qualities veterans possess" (3), including their "considerable experience with writing" (7), but they also solidified their partnership with the Veterans Advisory Council on their campus.

While the Certifying Official and the VRO can be excellent resources, faculty should not discount the impact they themselves have on a student veteran's experiences on campus—especially if those student veterans are enrolled in a writing class in their first semester. As David Vacchi and Joseph Berger note, "if a veteran experiences good faculty relationships for the first semester on campus, this will facilitate a smooth transition to college" (134).

In fact, Kristin Wilson et al. found that among the student veterans they interviewed, "their primary or sole connection to college was through their relationships with faculty" (640). One way to improve these relationships with faculty is to provide training. According to Nicholas Osborne, "[o]ffering faculty and staff development programs on veterans' issues, particularly in areas related to military culture and the limiting stereotypes that focus disproportionately on violence and trauma" are considered "essential for creating a veteran-friendly campus" (254)—or, by extension, a veteran-friendly writing classroom.[8]

Conclusion

Assets and Avenues

SOME OF THE NOTICEABLE SURGE OF student veterans appears to have waned since the launch of this project, but in truth, it has only changed. GI Bill education benefits will continue to be used for the next two decades at least, and in many instances in the coming years they will be used not by the veterans themselves, but by the veterans' family members. Children of today's service members are already using benefits, but as young service members' children mature into adulthood, many will find opportunities to go to college under the generosity of the Forever GI Bill.[1]

This fact points us to a few closing thoughts for WPAs and writing faculty to consider. The first is that training for faculty and staff and engagement with student veterans on campuses needs to continue to expand and change. Outreach is essential, and though we have tried to insist that not all institutions need to develop a plan for facilitating student veteran success, many do, and many still need to recognize the broad benefits of having a vibrant student veteran community on their campuses. Second, that outreach needs to start to more deliberately consider the changing demographics of those who will be using GI Bill benefits. Certainly, the military will continue to diversify, and those diverse groups of veterans will continue to seek out the promises of higher education. Spouses and family members, however, are and will continue in increasing numbers to use the benefits, and they will themselves bring distinct needs,

Portions of this chapter are borrowed or modified from our previously published essay "Veterans in the Writing Classroom," which appeared in *College Composition and Communication,* vol. 68, no. 2, Dec. 2016, pp. 345–71.

backgrounds, strengths, and challenges. Training and opportunities for faculty-student engagement will be crucial if those student populations are to feel at home in higher education.

Throughout our research, we repeatedly encountered anxiety among WPAs or veterans services staff concerning professional development about veterans on campus. The sense was that forcing (or even inviting) faculty to be prepared for "yet another professional development session to help students by modifying their classroom practices" would create more work for those conducting the professional development as well as resentment among those receiving it. Such concerns are not groundless, as overburdened faculty and staff may question the need for more training: "Why add more professional development workshops?"

We submit three answers to this question.

The first is that for many programs, specialized professional development on veterans' issues is unnecessary. WPAs and writing faculty should base their decisions on relevant data collected on their local campuses. As we note in the "Heuristics for WPAs and Writing Faculty Working with Veteran Populations" in the Writing/Practices Interchapter 2, thoughtful questions can provide avenues for gathering those data:

- How many student veterans are on campus (not just how many are receiving educational benefits)?
- How many are undergraduate students? Transfer students? Graduate students? Faculty? Staff?
- How many are veterans of the US military? Other countries' militaries?
- Is the campus near a military site or in a community with a historical military presence?
- How many dependents of service members and veterans are likely to be on campus?
- What professional development is already being conducted by a VSO?
- Is there an SVA chapter?
- Is there an ROTC presence?

These kinds of questions can help WPAs shape a local response to the national student veteran surge, and while not every campus will need to formulate a response, we maintain that program administrators in core fields such as writing have, in Marilyn Valentino's words in her 2010 CCCC Chair's Address, an "ethical obligation" to investigate and determine the level of need. National data amply illustrate why WPAs have that obligation, even if the response to that data will vary considerably from campus to campus.

When local circumstances demonstrate need for professional development, we would argue that a second reason to provide training is that an asset-based approach to education allows teachers to strengthen their classrooms by recognizing the values veterans bring to class. According to a report prepared by Greenberg Quinlan Rosner Research, presenting post-9/11 veterans in an "asset" frame[2] "produces an even better [perception] than portraying veterans as heroic. It also begins to reorient the way people think about how best to 'thank' veterans returning from service by shifting the focus from charity [or accommodation] to opportunity" (Lieberman and Stewart). However, as we mentioned earlier, virtually every professional development module or program we encountered focused on veteran "deficits": PTSD, TBI, trauma, lack of preparedness for college, absenteeism, disability, substance abuse, gender discrimination, sexual assault, transition issues. Such a deficit-based approach, we suggest, creates "a priori expectations about a student," which, as Eugenia Weiss explains, "can lead an educator to treat the student differently and in accord with those expectations." As a result, "students are likely to respond accordingly, regardless of their intellectual ability" (120). While the effects of military service during a time of active warfare are real and may require significant interventions,[3] they do not exclusively or even primarily constitute the student veteran experience. As Pamela Woll makes clear, "the subject of war and its effects can easily tip over into a dramatic focus on the negative or a stereotypical portrait of service members and veterans as dangerous, unstable, or objects of sympathy. The best focus will emphasize respect for these individuals . . . and belief in their strength and potential" (24).

Indeed, our research on writing pedagogy and student veterans affirms what other studies demonstrate: veterans tend to be an asset to the classroom. Many bring broad worldviews to complex issues, and all members of the military receive extensive training in leadership and team building. Further, promotion within the military is often linked to education and professional development, so that a veteran's capacity for learning per se is less of a hurdle than is the need for them to learn to adjust already well-developed learning processes to the relatively unfamiliar learning environment of the college classroom (see Chapter 3). Therefore, when faculty approach veterans as experts in their own fields—as highly trained professionals seeking to become proficient in new ways of knowing and learning—the significant assets of military students can strengthen classroom dynamics. In a 2014 op-ed, Mark Street points out that "in an academic community we are all there to question our own assumptions, to be surprised, and to be willing to let another's viewpoint or reaction challenge our own," which is why he appreciates how student veterans "enliven [his] classes . . . day to day." Erin Hadlock and Sue Doe also call attention to student veterans' "aptitude, agency, and critical thinking, all of which situate them to thrive in higher-education settings" (74). Among our interviewees, one of the most often-repeated sentiments was that faculty highly valued student veterans because of their professionalism, motivation, varied experiences, and maturity.

Emphasizing assets is at the heart of our third and final reason for including consideration of veterans in faculty professional development: WPAs should regard asset-based pedagogy as a research model. Such research traditionally centers on issues of educational justice in K–12 schools. As Django Paris and Samy Alim explain, "the vast majority of asset pedagogy research and practice has focused on the racialized and culturally situated heritage practices of [Indigenous American and African American] communities" (90). While we do not mean to suggest that the culturally situated practices of (former) military members are equivalent to the culturally situated heritage practices of marginalized student populations such as Indigenous Americans and African Americans, groups whose histories include military action and genocide against them, we concur with Lew Zipin that teaching and learning become more difficult when "learners' culturally inherited ways of knowing do not match those privileged in school curriculum" (317). For student veterans, this may mean a shift from action- and mission-oriented training to less immediately concrete educational objectives.

As Angie Mallory and Doug Downs note in their chapter in the collection *Generation Vet,* student veterans typically "do not cast [their military habits] aside. For example, every veteran [they] interviewed reported following the military script of showing up to a scheduled event (class) fifteen minutes early—to find no one else there" (61). Other student veterans shared with Mallory and Downs their initial dismay at what they perceived to be slovenliness in the dressing habits or physical postures of their professors and fellow classmates,[4] or the apparent lack of respect students demonstrated by calling a professor by their first name. These elements of academic culture can be unsettling to student veterans. By making an effort to "design curriculum that makes meaningful connections with ways of knowing in learners' lives beyond school . . . that is, to become open to learning about and from the lives of others, with conviction that these lives embody both intelligence and knowledge assets," writing instructors can potentially create a "more egalitarian, democratic and intellectually rich curriculum that puts diverse lifeworld learning assets to use" (Zipin 317–19). In asset-based frameworks, like those proposed by John Saltmarsh, "student's assets are embraced because the experience and knowledge they contribute to the learning process, and the authority of the knowledge they possess, contribute necessarily to the construction of new knowledge" (342). As former Marine and current college writing instructor Galen Leonhardy reminds us, "we have much to learn" from student veterans (342).

As we discussed earlier in this volume, Corrine Hinton's research on Marine Corps student veterans shows that those "who [are] able to identify and then translate previous learning and rhetorical experiences from the military into academic writing contexts [are more likely to report] positive perceptions about that writing" ("Military"), and Cathleen Morreale has similarly argued that

> the educational quality of military students can be improved through the development of socio-educational relationships . . . such as recognizing a student's knowledge by having them provide spontaneous accounts, presenting alternative versions of arguments, engaging various participants holding contradictory opinions, building arguments collectively through work in small groups. (138)

By setting aside preconceptions and guiding student veterans to recognize similarities between academic writing and military writing, we help them "identify and unpack the kinds of action agency that were valued in the military and compare these to the kinds of learning and writing agency that will be needed in college classrooms" (Hadlock and Doe 90).

This is all to say that veterans' lived experiences promise to help shape classroom discussions, and their professional writing experiences stand to enrich students' considerations of various academic and nonacademic literacies. Prompting dialogue about what helps veterans on a particular campus learn better will, we believe, prompt greater engagement with different ways of knowing and seeing the world, and such epistemological discussions may consequently help transform our ways of approaching our writing classrooms. Acknowledging student veterans' needs while also recognizing their assets not only helps us to enact good pedagogy, but it is also at the very heart of the veteran ethos: service. In this case, to our students.

NOTES

Foreword

1. In sociological terms, being a veteran is characterized as an achieved status, not an ascribed status.

Introduction: Theorizing the Post-9/11 Veteran

1. According to the College Board website, credit for successfully completed CLEP exams is awarded "at 2,900 U.S. colleges and universities." The website also has a prominent link to "Military Benefits," which informs readers that "[b]ecause the exams are funded by the United States government through the Defense Activity for Non-Traditional Education Support (DANTES) . . . [e]ach year, nearly 50,000 military service members from the Army, Navy, U.S. Air Force and U.S. Coast Guard, as well as eligible spouses and civil service employees, take CLEP exams to reach their education goals" ("Military Benefits").

2. In 2017, according to the Veterans Benefits Administration *Annual Benefits Report Fiscal Year 2017,* only 9 percent of veterans applied their education benefits to graduate degree programs.

3. For example, in 2017, "Veterans Affairs Secretary David Shulkin took exception to describing the Texas church shooter as a veteran, because he was given a bad conduct discharge" (Shane).

4. See Army veteran Zach Trzinski's essay "Not All Veterans Are the Same" for a perspective from a student veteran who served in Afghanistan in 2012.

5. Similarly, an Association for the Study of Higher Education (ASHE) report notes, "Although a number of students may be challenged by adapting to the college environment, particularly if they function in additional roles such as parent, worker, and caregiver, the status of student veteran adds yet another layer to the complexity of intersecting identities. In addition to the social identities of race, culture, sexual orientation, and gender, other preentry variables such

as first-generation status, officer or enlisted rank, socioeconomic status, and disability all differentially affect the veteran as he or she enters the academy" (Braxton 56).

6. In her study of student veterans and "military friendly" campuses, Ellen Moore critiques the "ideology of military superiority" on campuses that "reduces military veterans to essential qualities of complexity, maturity, and toughness" and has the effect of "creat[ing] barriers between veterans and their civilian classmates" (80).

7. In a January 2019 NPR interview, for example, General Frank Muth, the head of the Army Recruiting Command, noted that "only a small percentage of those in the Army directly participate in active land combat. The rest work in a variety of around 150 different jobs" (Fadel and Morris).

8. The Moral Injury Project at Syracuse University defines moral injury as "the damage done to one's conscience or moral compass when that person perpetrates, witnesses, or fails to prevent acts that transgress their own moral and ethical values or codes of conduct" ("What Is").

9. For a more detailed description of our research methods, please see our white paper, "An Ethical Obligation."

1. Writing (Veterans) Studies

1. Compare this to the fact that "[d]uring World War II, *College English* published [just] four articles (February 1944, May 1944, March 1945, May 1945) explicitly concerned with connections between literacy instruction in higher education and the contemporary military" (Edwards and Hart).

2. The text of DoD Directive 1304.26 reads, "A person's sexual orientation is considered a personal and private matter, and is not a bar to service entry or continued service unless manifested by homosexual conduct. . . . Applicants for enlistment, appointment, or induction shall not be asked or required to reveal whether they are heterosexual, homosexual or bisexual."

2. The Rhetoric of the GI Bill

1. The Post-9/11 GI Bill is now known as the Forever GI Bill as a result of the passage of the 2017 Harry W. Colmery Veterans Educational Assistance Act.

2. For example, the Executive Committee of the Conference on College Composition and Communication (CCCC) passed the following resolution in March 2003:

WHEREAS in our best moments we have relied on the power of rhetoric to mediate disputes, and in our college classrooms we teach students to understand one another, respect their differences, and resolve their disputes through discourse; BE IT THEREFORE RESOLVED that we encourage teachers of writing and communication at colleges and universities across the country to engage students and others in learning and debate about the issues and implications of the Iraqi war and any other acts of war perpetrated by the United States of America. ("Resolution")

3. Literary scholar Patrick Deer also criticizes what he describes as "the sacralization of the figure of the veteran" (70) as well as "the ways in which a war culture both reveals and conceals, producing a surge in violent imagery and rhetoric that enforces a sense of commonality while simultaneously silencing, compartmentalizing, and excluding dissenting perspectives" (56).

4. While the GI Bill was "the first explicitly race-neutral piece of social legislation" and by 1950 49 percent of black veterans "had used the G.I. Bill for education or training of some sort" as compared to 43 percent of white veterans, we must acknowledge that the bill was passed into law in a country that was still segregated and therefore "when it came to the key benefits of home loans and college education . . . black veterans clearly fell behind" (Humes 93–94), particularly those who lived in the southern states (Turner and Bound).

5. It is worth noting that "advances in emergency medicine and quick access to state-of-the-art medical facilities have dramatically increased the chances that a soldier will survive a battlefield wound. . . . Expressed in a different way, troops fighting in Iraq and Afghanistan survive nearly 90% of all combat injuries, compared with 72% in Vietnam and 63% in World War II" (*Military-Civilian Gap* 74). Even so, "The Iraq and Afghanistan wars account for over 50,500 reported physical injuries; 20% involve spinal cord and brain injury, and 6% result in amputation . . . [and] [a]pproximately 10% of veteran-documented disabilities are hearing impairments including tinnitus, hearing loss, and otitis media" (Graf, Ysasi, and Marini 19).

6. While the GI Bill is most often thought of as providing benefits for higher education, it was deliberately designed to allow veterans to use the benefits "for any educational or training programs to which they were accepted. G.I. benefits not only covered enrollment at

colleges and universities but also provided opportunities for vocational, technical, and apprenticeship training. In fact, the majority of veterans who received training under the World War II G.I. Bill participated in noncollegiate and on-the-job programs" (Turner and Bound 149).

7. Not all eligible veterans were afforded equal access to the benefits of social and civic advancement, however. As Hilary Herbold notes, "Overcrowding at the historically black institutions of the South, and discriminatory admissions policies at other colleges and universities, meant that for many [black] veterans in search of a college degree, vocational training programs and trade schools were the only available options" (107). To make matters worse, "the locally appointed, white veterans officials in charge of vocational benefits and on-the-job training programs, particularly in the Jim Crow South, directed black veterans away from highly paid, skilled work in the private sector, and toward menial, unskilled, low-wage positions" (Humes 97).

8. The GI Bill changed the curriculum of HBCUs, as well: "[T]he arrival of veterans forced the HBCUs to expand or, in many cases, to form departments outside the disciplines of pedagogy and the church. The effect of the bill on black colleges, then, was similar to its impact on white institutions insofar as it effected a shift in educational philosophy. But at the HBCUs the transition to a curriculum beyond preaching and teaching took place slowly, in part because employment in technical and scientific fields was still largely closed to blacks. It made little sense to pursue a degree in electronics if industry continued to confine blacks to unskilled jobs" (Herbold 108).

9. In his article, Giroux asks, "How might educators and others engage pedagogical practices that open up spaces of resistance to neoliberal/militarized modes of governance and authority through a culture of questioning that enables people to resist and reject neoliberal assumptions that reduce masculinity to expressions of military valor, values and battle? What are the implications of theorizing pedagogy and the practice of learning as essential to social change and where might such interventions take place? How might the related matters of experience and learning, knowledge and authority, and history and cultural capital be theorized as part of a broader pedagogy of critique and possibility?" (73). We suggest that many professors in writing studies are enacting these pedagogical practices daily.

3. Transferring Veteran Knowledge

1. In his interviews with student veterans, Mark Blaauw-Hara noted that several veterans "highlighted the military's emphasis on completing the mission as a principal strength of student veterans. In the academic context, completing the mission could mean completing an assignment, class, or degree program, a connection between the military and academic worlds several veterans made explicitly" ("Military" 812).

2. DiRamio, Ackerman, and Mitchell also found that for many of the veterans with whom they spoke, "the transition [they] make when they become college students . . . was the most difficult transition of all" ("Transitions" 8). Vacchi similarly argues that "one of the most awkward places for a student veteran to be after military service is on a college campus" (18).

3. In regard to registration, at some institutions, participants said that the courses required by their degree plans filled up quickly, and there were not enough sections to accommodate everyone who needed the course. As a result, some veterans were reportedly unable to take all the credits they needed in a given term to stay on track to graduate within the thirty-six months allowed by the various GI bills (Steele, Salcedo, and Coley 24).

4. "From 2008 through 2010, SVA focused on expanding and supporting the network of chapters. This included assisting in the development of new chapters, while also supporting existing ones. The result was an astonishing growth rate for SVA. For example, SVA was founded with only 20 chapters and in 2011, SVA welcomed its 500th chapter" ("About Us").

5. SVA chapters are much more prevalent on four-year campuses. As a student veteran at one community college explained, "The problem is, with the turnover rate . . . it's hard to keep [an SVA organization] going." In other words, "lack of continuity among students at the school meant that an organization could not sustain itself over time" (Griffin and Gilbert 88–89).

6. Vacchi and Berger also found that "a significant percentage of those student veterans attending community colleges continue on to four-year colleges" (112), as did the Million Records Project (Cate 33).

7. As Alvarez notes, many veterans choose to enroll in two-year colleges because they "offer flexible class schedules, enroll older students and can feel less intimidating—all important issues to veterans, who are usually older and often married with families."

8. "With the exception of those enrolled at the community colleges, the veterans perceived themselves as having little in common with other undergraduate students" (Griffin and Gilbert 88).

9. According to the National Center for Educational Statistics: "Nontraditional status is based on the presence of one or more of seven possible nontraditional characteristics. These characteristics include older than typical age, part-time attendance, being independent of parents, working full time while enrolled, having dependents, being a single parent, and being a recipient of a GED or high school completion certificate" ("Nontraditional").

10. As one student veteran remarked, military members are "used to a tight knit community, but [on campus] it's like you're an island. . . . I miss that camaraderie" (Olsen, Badger, and McCuddy 104).

11. As Griffin and Gilbert point out, "there can be great diversity within the student veteran population, and other identities and responsibilities may be more salient than one's military experiences. While some may feel their identity as a veteran is salient and want to connect to others with similar experiences, others may perceive their transition as being more similar to others entering higher education" (92).

12. In her 2016 dissertation, Karina Money drew a similar conclusion: "Interviews with those that work directly with students to support their success reveal that active duty military and student veterans are often the best prepared academically. The difficulty lies in finding ways to help these students translate the skills and attitudes they have developed through their military service into the academic setting" (46).

13. As Erin Hadlock notes, "as active duty soldiers, student-veterans used many of the rhetorical skills taught in a composition classroom but often have difficulty recognizing what they did as *writing*" (iii, emphasis in original), which confirms the need for prompting student veterans to that recognition.

14. Hinton's findings are echoed in the findings of Eodice, Geller, and Lerner in *The Meaningful Writing Project*.

15. "Military members acquired time management skills, confidence in themselves during challenging circumstances, cognitive flexibility when solving problems or evaluating information, and openness to diversity. Much of this governed their behavior in the college environment" (Stone 382).

16. Gregg, Howell, and Shordike found that the participants in their study "began their transition by repurposing individual traits and

skills cultivated in the military to support their new role as a student. For many, this process required reflection on both positive and negative military experiences that guided the transition. Military principles grounded in accountability and discipline resonated with participants as they incorporated the traits learned in the military into the educational context" (3). However, other "accomplishments achieved in the military were of limited value in [the] new context" (4).

17. Griffin and Gilbert also discovered "a lack of consistent interest in connecting socially" among the student veterans they interviewed (92).

18. "[Fifty-one] percent of undergraduates aged 25 or older attend community colleges" (*College Students Today*).

19. "[Sixty-nine] percent of undergraduates aged 25 or older are married and/or have children" (*College Students Today*), while "62 percent" of undergraduate student veterans aged twenty-four or older have "a spouse, child, or both" (Radford 7).

20. Michelle Navarre Cleary's research on adult students demonstrates that "[a]nxiety about how school works is intensified in writing classes for those adult students who discover that what they remember about academic writing has lost currency. . . . Writing process methods, kinds of assignments, citations methods and the nature of sources have all changed since many adults were in school. As a result, writing classes can be sites of extreme, potentially paralyzing anxiety for them" (116).

21. For-profit institutions and online institutions provide significant benefits to veterans, such as twelve-month programs, no breaks in benefits, and flexibility in scheduling. Indeed, many service members take courses while deployed, even in combat zones. Nonetheless, our research was limited to two-year and four-year traditional institutions.

22. Similarly, all of the student veterans Wheeler interviewed indicated that their service experiences "positively influenced their academic experience" (782).

23. As Wheeler notes, "Coming from a culture where the chain of command is paramount and respect is a requirement, students who talk in class, text message, don't take notes, or fall asleep offend and anger veterans who have been trained to focus on the task at hand and respect authority," and younger students' "lack of appreciation for 'anything' while complaining about 'everything' [is] insulting to veterans who have been in a war zone" (784).

24. Devitt is concerned that "transfer" as an idea or organizing principle is itself too broad to be taken seriously. Instead, she argues that a focus on genre would be more useful in helping students connect modes of writing to other contexts. Such a view, of course, assumes that genres themselves are somehow more widely applicable than rhetorical principles such as understanding of audience or clarifying purpose.

4. Developing Veteran-Informed Classrooms

1. In our 2010 survey of WPAs and writing instructors, 44.2 percent of respondents (some of whom represent the same institutions) stated that they had noticed an increase of student veterans in their writing classes.

2. In the same survey, 62.3 percent of respondents stated that their FYW classes are capped at between twenty and twenty-five students, while 23.8 percent had caps between fifteen and twenty students. Only 10.8 percent of respondents had caps of more than twenty-five. We also want to note here that we deliberately used the term *classmates* rather than *peers,* as many student veterans would not identify their classmates as their peers due to differences in age and experience.

3. In the same survey, 71 percent of respondents indicated that FYW classes at their institutions "typically include assignments of personal narrative essays." Similarly, 69.5 percent of respondents concurred that some form of "journal" is assigned in FYW.

4. During our research, we learned that during the Vietnam era, faculty members at some institutions were provided with class rosters that *did* indicate which, if any, of their students were receiving educational benefits from the military. According to our sources, this practice was instituted in order to "catch" veterans who were cashing in on their benefits without actually attending classes or working toward degree completion. A 1978 article in *The Atlantic* points out that "by 1977, only 30 percent of the Vietnam-era veterans without a high school education had used any part of their G.I. Bill benefits. And, of course, there [was] no way of telling how many Vietnam veterans [used] the Bill [which was distributed in monthly lump sum payments to cover tuition only], not primarily to go to school and learn a trade, but to get cash and keep themselves and their families in food" (Kidder).

5. While we don't want to downplay the significant impact of post-traumatic stress disorder (PTSD) and traumatic brain injury

(TBI)—the "signature wounds" of the most recent wars, we also want to make it clear that according to the Pew Research Center's 2011 report *The Military-Civilian Gap: War and Sacrifice in the Post-9/11 Era,* the Veterans Administration (VA) has stated that only 11 to 20 percent of OIF/OEF veterans have been diagnosed with PTSD, although 37 percent believe they have suffered from it, whether diagnosed or not (1). According to a report by the RAND Corporation, 20 percent of OIF/OEF veterans have PTSD, while 19 percent have TBI (Tanielian et al.).

6. As retired Army Captain Shannon Meehan has argued, "The stories we tell consistently portray veterans in extremes—either emphasizing vets' heroism beyond comprehension or their propensity for erratic violence. . . . Because of the unreal, formulaic depictions of vets in our culture, [veterans] remain distanced from society, leaving little chance that anyone will actually see [vets] as real people with both strengths and struggles."

7. In response to the question, "Do first-year writing classes at your institution typically include assignments of personal narrative essays?" 71.3 percent of respondents to our survey answered "Yes," with 5.4 percent answering, "Don't know."

8. See Hart and Thompson ("War, Trauma") for discussion of women as outsiders in the military (42–45).

9. Former Marine and current two-year college writing professor Galen Leonhardy, for example, suggests that we should be open to offering veterans opportunities to explore their military experiences (and, indeed, research shows that many student veterans appreciate the opportunity to write about VA benefits—whether educational or medical—about veteran homelessness, etc.). We should not, however, require or expect them to do so.

10. We concur with Sarah Roff with regard to "trigger warnings": "Since triggers are a contagious phenomenon, there will never be enough trigger warnings to keep up with them. It should not be the job of college educators to foster this process. It would be *much more useful for faculty members and students to be trained how to respond* if they are concerned that a student or peer has suffered trauma" (emphasis added). See also Valentino ("Serving") on considerations to take into account when deciding whether or not to assign readings, films, and essays on war.

11. In her book *Grateful Nation*, Ellen Moore shares the story of Mitchell, a student veteran who "came to believe that it was important

for him [to] talk about the war with his civilian classmates [in an English class]. He wanted to educate them about an issue he considered vitally important and to make his combat experience visible and comprehensible" (179), but Moore acknowledges that "this moment highlights a dilemma veterans face trying to bridge the experiential divide between civilians and military: many veterans feel the need to educate civilians, to make them understand the human costs of war, but this effort to educate [comes] at an emotional cost" (181).

12. Such as, for example, recognizing that most students participating in the Reserve Officers Training Corps (ROTC) do not have veteran status and have not been deployed.

5. Engaging Veteran Trauma

1. In their systematic review of "the data-based peer-reviewed research examining student service members/veterans (SSM/V) in higher education" (30), Adam Barry, Shawn Whiteman, and Shelley Mac-Dermid Wadsworth found that "[e]arlier research contrasting veteran students participating in higher education with nonveterans focused primarily on scholastics, such as academic achievement and associated outcomes. Of those studies, the vast majority found student service members/veterans from the WWII era and Vietnam era to outperform their civilian counterparts academically" (31).

2. Three hundred eighteen of the 446 respondents (or 71.3 percent) answered "yes" to the question "Do first-year writing classes at your institution typically include assignments of personal narrative essays?" Three hundred ten (or 69.5 percent) responded "yes" to the question, "Do first-year writing classes at your institution typically include assignments of journals or blogs?"

3. We have written elsewhere, for example, about the use of the word *perpetrated* in the CCCC's Resolution encouraging "teachers of writing and communication at colleges and universities across the country to engage students and others in learning and debate about the issues and implications of the Iraqi war and any other acts of war perpetrated by the United States of America" (Hart and Thompson, "From").

4. Out of 446 respondents to our survey, almost 70 percent stated that their department or program had *not* discussed in a formal way, either in department meetings or committee meetings or other formal settings, the effect of veterans in the writing classroom.

Writing/Practices 2

1. For example, the CCCC Position Statement "Student Veterans in the College Composition Classroom: Realizing Their Strengths and Assessing Their Needs" deliberately avoids the language of "best practices."

2. According to research done by the American Council on Education, "a majority of [undergraduate] veterans are enrolled in community colleges [38 percent] and for-profit colleges [23 percent]" (Molina). See also Sewall.

3. In the 2016 SVA survey, the highest numbers of respondents were located in states with numerous military installations such as California, Texas, Washington, and Virginia (Cate and Davis).

4. In fact, "'educational benefits' was the most commonly cited reason for joining the military in the beginning of the Global War on Terror," resulting in "[f]orty-five percent of all GWT veterans under the age of 30 [attending] college as either full-time or part-time students since 2011" since "[f]or many of the 2.3 million veterans returning from the conflicts in Afghanistan and Iraq, going to college has been a popular method of reintegration" (Naphan and Elliot 36).

5. Nine out of ten respondents in the 2016 SVA survey "indicated that they were enlisted service members during their military service. Of the remaining 9.65 percent, 1.20 percent were warrant officers and the remaining 8.45 percent were commissioned officers" (Cate and Davis 4). Of post-9/11 student veterans, 82 percent are enlisted ("I Am" 2).

6. As Osborne points out, student veterans' organizations "provide integral opportunities to hear firsthand of veterans' experiences with academic and social transitions and to hear about their perceptions of the institutional climate" (250). Therefore, WPAs may want to coordinate with their VROs in order to have a chance to speak to and invite members of the student veterans' organizations to share their stories with writing faculty.

7. See Wright's master's thesis, "Improvise, Adapt, and Overcome: The Student Veteran and Considerations of Identity, Space, and Pedagogy," for a more thorough description of the Writing Center Tutor Corps at Texas State.

8. As Kristin Wilson et al. found through their interviews with student veterans, "the important issue for faculty, outside of content knowledge, becomes one of building relationships (e.g., mentoring)

with this student population. A couple of the participants identified instructors with an understanding of military culture by their willingness to be flexible when the soldier was deployed or placed on a temporary duty assignment. Professional development for faculty aimed at understanding nuances associated with a life in service to the military (e.g., common language used, deployments, rank structure) may be a way to help faculty create inviting learning environments" (640).

Conclusion

1. "The fact that the current G.I. Bill affords educational opportunities to family members of veterans will also ensure ongoing military-affiliated student enrollment growth ("Transfer"). The implications of shared benefits are far-reaching. First, they remind us that our classrooms contain not only veterans, but also spouses and children of veterans. In communities with high numbers of National Guard members or reservists, this may be especially true, as those veteran populations tend to be older and often already have families and grown children. Additionally, the extension of educational benefits to family members means those who have been deeply connected to OIF and OEF will continue to appear in our classrooms for generations. Military dependents—many of whom will have been significantly impacted by the length and severity of two concurrent wars—will enroll in college up to two decades from now, and, as ample research testifies, they will be bringing with them the generational costs of war. . . . The evidence that the legacy of war is passed from veterans to children is overwhelming, and while here we use *cost* in the broadest possible way, the monetary costs for war are no less real. For examples of studies on the emotional costs, see Motta et al.; Dahl, McCubbin, and Ross; Scharf; Dekel and Goldblatt. For an accessible and personal account of the generational effects of war, see Levinson. [Leila] Levinson has coordinated writing groups for veterans and their families in the Austin area, and she has taught war literature and writing at several colleges" (Hart and Thompson, "Veterans in Writing Classes" 347 and footnote).

2. Similarly, Eileen Schell and Ivy Kleinbart encourage veteran writers outside of a classroom context "to think about how their military training is an asset" when it comes to "the act of writing" (137).

3. For example, in her *Generation Vet* chapter "Faculty as First Responders," Linda De La Ysla, whose student Charles Whittington

published his essay "War Is a Drug" in the college newspaper and who never completed his degree after being told by school officials that he would not be allowed on campus until he had a psychological evaluation, acknowledges her lack of preparation for "what to do or what to say" and points out that "many teachers of writing" also lack clarity about how to provide "supportive and pedagogically sound responses" when confronted with veterans' narratives of trauma (97). Reflecting on the situation, De La Ysla concluded that "faculty [need] to recognize the existence of student-veterans as a distinct yet heterogeneous group . . . and realize that within that diversity [are] individuals [who are] suffering," and that writing teachers need "to be aware of whatever resources [exist] on campus as well as off" (110).

4. Indeed, one of the many concerns expressed in our survey was how to productively engage student veterans with their civilian classmates. According to Eugenia Weiss, faculty members who strive to promote "safety and community in the classroom . . . should do all they can to foster student-to-student connections in a nonthreatening and culturally responsive manner." She cites Allport's Intergroup Contact Theory as a "starting point" (116).

WORKS CITED

"About Us." Student Veterans of America, studentveterans.org/aboutus.

Ackerman, Robert, and David DiRamio, editors. *Creating a Veteran-Friendly Campus: Strategies for Transition and Success.* New Directions for Student Services No. 126. Jossey-Bass, 2009.

———. "Transitions: Combat Veterans as College Students." Ackerman and DiRamio, pp. 5–14.

Aldridge, Delores P., and Carlene Young, editors. *Out of the Revolution: The Development of Africana Studies.* Lexington Books, 2000.

Alvarez, Lizette. "Combat to College." *New York Times,* Education Life Supplement, 30 Oct. 2008, pp. 24+.

Annual Benefits Report Fiscal Year 2017. US Department of Veterans Affairs, Veterans Benefits Administration, www.benefits.va.gov/RE PORTS/abr/docs/2017_abr.pdf.

Anson, Chris M., and Jessie L. Moore. Introduction. *Critical Transitions: Writing and the Question of Transfer,* edited by Anson and Moore, WAC Clearinghouse and UP of Colorado, 2017, pp. 3–13.

Anson, Chris, and Shawn Neely. "The Army as Textual Community: Exploring Mismatches in the Concepts of Attribution, Appropriation, and Shared Goals." *Kairos,* vol. 14, no. 3, Summer 2010.

"Army Writing Style." US Army Combined Arms Center, 19 Dec. 2013, https://usacac.army.mil/cac2/wocc/ArmyWritingStyle.asp.

Baechtold, Margaret, and Danielle M. De Sawal. "Meeting the Needs of Women Veterans." Ackerman and DiRamio, pp. 35–43.

Barnet, Sylvan and Hugo Bedau. *Current Issues and Enduring Questions.* 10th ed. Macmillan Education, 2014.

Barr, Meghan. "Teacher's Mission: Guide Vets Back to Campus." *San Diego Union Tribune,* 4 July 2009, www.sandiegouniontribune.com/sdut-us-combat-campus-070409-2009jul04-story.html.

Barry, Adam E., Shawn D. Whiteman, and Shelley MacDermid Wadsworth. "Student Service Members/Veterans in Higher Education: A

Systematic Review." *Journal of Student Affairs Research and Practice,* vol. 51, no. 1, 2014, pp. 30–42.

Bauman, Mark. "The Mobilization and Return of Undergraduate Students Serving in the National Guard and Reserves." Ackerman and DiRamio, pp. 15–23.

Beaufort, Anne. *College Writing and Beyond: A New Framework for University Writing Instruction.* Utah State UP, 2007.

Belkin, Aaron, et al. "Readiness and DADT Repeal: Has the New Policy of Open Service Undermined the Military?" *Armed Forces & Society,* vol. 39, no. 4, Oct. 2013, pp. 587–601.

Benedict, Helen. *The Lonely Soldier: The Private War of Women Serving in Iraq.* Beacon Press, 2009.

Berrett, Dan. "Words from Wartime." *Inside Higher Ed,* 8 Apr. 2011, www.insidehighered.com/news/2011/04/08/words-wartime.

Biank, Tanya. *Undaunted: The Real Story of America's Servicewomen in Today's Military.* New American Library, 2014.

Bird, Caroline. "College Is a Waste of Time and Money." 1975. *Known Stalkers,* knownstalkers.com/info%20pages/CollegeWaste.pdf. Accessed 10 Nov. 2019.

Blaauw-Hara, Mark. "'Learning Shock' and Student Veterans: Bridging the Learning Environments of the Military and the Academy." *Composition Forum,* vol. 35, 2017.

———. "'The Military Taught Me How to Study, How to Work Hard': Helping Student-Veterans Transition by Building on Their Strengths." *Community College Journal of Research and Practice,* vol. 40, no. 10, 2016, pp. 809–23.

Black, Richard. "Fifty Years of Refugee Studies: From Theory to Policy." *International Migration Review,* vol. 35, no. 1, 2001, pp. 57–78.

Blanton, Rebecca, and Lisa K. Foster. *California's Women Veterans: Responses to the 2011 Survey.* California Research Bureau, July 2012, www.library.ca.gov/Content/pdf/crb/reports/12-004.pdf.

Bonar, Ted C., and Paula L. Domenici. "Counseling and Connecting with the Military Undergraduate: The Intersection of Military Service and University Life." *Journal of College Student Psychotherapy,* vol. 25, no. 3, 2011, pp. 204–19.

Boone, Stephanie, et al. "Imagining a Writing and Rhetoric Program Based on Principles of Knowledge 'Transfer': Dartmouth's Institute of Writing and Rhetoric." *Composition Forum,* vol. 26, 2012.

Born of Controversy: The G.I. Bill of Rights. US Department of Veterans Affairs, www.va.gov/opa/publications/celebrate/gi-bill.pdf.

Borsari, Brian, et al. "Student Service Members/Veterans on Campus: Challenges for Reintegration." *American Journal of Orthopsychiatry,* vol. 87, no. 2, 2017, pp. 166–75.

Bousquet, Marc. "Composition as Management Science." *Tenured Bosses and Disposable Teachers: Writing Instruction in the Managed University,* edited by Bousquet, Tony Scott, and Leo Parascondola. Southern Illinois UP, 2004, pp. 11–35.

Bradshaw, Crystal. "The Importance of Effective Writing in the NCO Corps." *NCO Journal,* 22 Sept. 2017.

Braxton, John M. "Crisis of Identity? Veteran, Civilian, Student." DiRamio and Jarvis, pp. 53–65.

Brent, Doug. "Transfer, Transformation, and Rhetorical Knowledge: Insights from Transfer Theory." *Journal of Business and Technical Communication,* vol. 25, no. 4, 2011, pp. 396–420.

Brodsky, Marc D., and Bruce E. Pencek. "Is the Library Ready for an Emerging Field? The Case of Veterans Studies." *Too Much Is Not Enough! Proceedings of the Charleston Library Conference,* edited by Beth R. Bernhardt, Leah H. Hinds, and Katina P. Strauch, Against the Grain P/Purdue UP, 2014, pp. 142–47.

Bronner, Michael. "The Recruiters' War." *Vanity Fair,* 1 Sept. 2005, www.vanityfair.com/news/2005/09/recruiters200509.

Burdick, Melanie. "Grading the War Story." *Teaching English in the Two-Year College,* vol. 36, no. 4, 2009, pp. 353–54.

Byron, Paula. "Summer Institute to Focus on Societal Perceptions and Self-Views of Veterans." *Virginia Tech News,* 5 May 2016, vtnews.vt.edu/articles/2016/05/clahs-summerinstituteveterans.html.

Calcagno, Juan Carlos, et al. "Community College Student Success: What Institutional Characteristics Make a Difference?" *Economics of Education Review,* vol. 27, no. 6, 2008, pp. 632–45.

Canfield, Julie, and Eugenia L. Weiss. "Student Veterans and Mental Health: Posttraumatic Stress in the Classroom." Coll and Weiss, pp. 260–87.

Carden, Michael J. "Program Helps Veterans Transition from War Zone to Campus." 10 Feb. 2009. US Department of Defense, archive.defense.gov/news/newsarticle.aspx?id=53022.

Carter, Michael. "Ways of Knowing, Doing, and Writing in the Disciplines." *College Composition and Communication,* vol. 58, no. 3, Feb. 2007, pp. 385–418.

Caruth, Cathy. *Unclaimed Experience: Trauma, Narrative, and History.* 20th anniversary ed. Johns Hopkins UP, 2016.

Cate, Chris A. *Million Records Project: Research from Student Veterans of America.* Student Veterans of America, 2014.

Cate, Chris A., and Taylor Davis. "Student Veteran Demographics: Select Results from Student Veterans of America Spotlight 2016." *SVA Spotlight,* vol. 2, no. 1, Feb. 2016.

Cate, Chris A., et al. *National Veteran Education Success Tracker: A Report on the Academic Success of Student Veterans Using the Post-9/11 GI Bill.* Student Veterans of America, 2017.

Center for Veteran Transition and Integration, Columbia University. veterans.columbia.edu/.

"Charles Whittington, Vet Who Wrote about Addiction to Violence, Barred from College." *Huffington Post,* 23 Nov. 2010, www.huffingtonpost.com/2010/11/23/charles-whittington-vet-w_n_787344.html.

Coll, Jose E., and Eugenia L. Weiss, editors. *Supporting Veterans in Higher Education: A Primer for Administrators, Faculty, and Advisors.* Lyceum Books, 2015.

College Students Today: A National Portrait. American Council on Education, 2005, www.acenet.edu/Documents/College-Students-Today-A-National-Portrait-2005.pdf.

Corley, Liam. "'Brave Words': Rehabilitating the Veteran-Writer." *College English,* vol. 74, no. 4, Mar. 2012, pp. 351–65.

Côté, James E., and Anton L. Allahar. *Lowering Higher Education: The Rise of Corporate Universities and the Fall of Liberal Education.* U of Toronto P, 2011.

Craig, Jim. "Bounding Veterans Studies: A Review of the Field." *Race and/or Reconciliation: Proceedings of the Third Conference on Veterans in Society,* edited by Heidi Nobles and Marcia Davitt, Virginia Tech U, 2016, pp. 101–18.

Crawley, Kristy Liles. "Renewing Our Commitment to Connecting to Student Veterans." *Teaching English in the Two-Year College,* vol. 41, no. 1, Sept. 2013, pp. 20–25.

Crowley, Helen. "Women's Studies: Between a Rock and a Hard Place or Just Another Cell in the Beehive?" *Feminist Review,* no. 61, 1999, pp. 131–50.

Dahl, Barbara, H. I. McCubbin, and K. L. Ross. "Second Generational Effects of War-Induced Separations: Comparing the Adjustment of Children in Reunited and Non-Reunited Families." National Council for Family Relations Annual Conference, 19–23 Aug. 1975, Salt Palace Hotel, Salt Lake City, UT.

Deer, Patrick. "Mapping Contemporary American War Culture." *College Literature,* vol. 43, no. 1, 2016, pp. 48–90.

Dekel, Rachel, and Hadass Goldblatt. "Is There Intergenerational Transmission of Trauma? The Case of Combat Veterans' Children." *American Journal of Orthopsychiatry,* vol. 78, no. 3, Jul. 2008, pp. 281–89.

De La Ysla, Linda S. "Faculty as First Responders: Willing but Unprepared." Doe and Langstraat, pp. 95–116.

Devitt, Amy. "Transferability and Genres." *The Locations of Composition,* edited by Christopher J. Keller and Christian R. Weisser. SUNY P, 2007, pp. 215–27.

DiRamio, David, editor. *What's Next for Student Veterans? Moving from Transition to Academic Success.* U of South Carolina, National Resource Center for the First-Year Experience and Students in Transition, 2017.

DiRamio, David, Robert Ackerman, and Regina L. Mitchell. "From Combat to Campus: Voices of Student-Veterans." *NASPA Journal,* vol. 45, no. 1, 2008, pp. 73–102.

DiRamio, David, and Kathryn Jarvis, editors. *Veterans in Higher Education: When Johnny and Jane Come Marching to Campus,* special issue of the *ASHE Higher Education Report* vol. 37, no. 3, 2011.

Doe, Sue, and William W. Doe III. "Residence Time and Military Workplace Literacies." *Composition Forum,* vol. 28, 2013.

Doe, Sue, and Lisa Langstraat, editors. *Generation Vet: Composition, Student-Veterans, and the Post-9/11 University.* UP of Colorado, 2014.

Doerries, Bryan, translator. *All That You've Seen Here Is God: New Versions of Four Greek Tragedies.* Vintage, 2015.

———. *The Theater of War: What Ancient Greek Tragedies Can Teach Us Today.* Knopf, 2016.

Dunbar, Laura. *Josephs of the Country: James Jones's Thirty-Year Men and the Image of the WWII Soldier in American Culture.* 2016. U of Toronto, PhD dissertation.

"Education." *FY 2013 Annual Benefits Report—Education Section.* US Department of Veterans Affairs, 26 Sept. 2014, www.benefits.va.gov/REPORTS/abr/docs/2013_abr.pdf.

Edwards, Mike, and Alexis Hart. "Logging On: Special Issue: Rhetoric, Technology, and the Military." *Kairos,* vol. 14, no. 3, Summer 2010.

Eichler, Maya. "Add Female Veterans and Stir? A Feminist Perspective on Gendering Veterans Research." *Armed Forces & Society,* vol. 43, no. 4, 2017, pp. 674–94.

Elbow, Peter. "Appendix Essay: The Doubting Game and the Believing Game—An Analysis of the Intellectual Enterprise." *Writing without Teachers,* by Elbow, Oxford UP, 1973, pp. 147–91.

Elliott, Marta, Carlene Gonzalez, and Barbara Larsen. "U.S. Military Veterans Transition to College: Combat, PTSD, and Alienation on Campus." *Journal of Student Affairs Research and Practice*, vol. 48, no. 3, 2011, pp. 279–96.

Eodice, Michele, Anne Ellen Geller, and Neal Lerner. *The Meaningful Writing Project: Learning, Teaching, and Writing in Higher Education.* UP of Colorado, 2016.

Fact Sheet: A College Degree: Surest Pathway to Expanded Opportunity, Success for American Students. US Department of Education, 16 Sept. 2016, www.ed.gov/news/press-releases/fact-sheet-college-degree-surest-pathway-expanded-opportunity-success-american-students.

Fadel, Leila, and Amanda Morris. "After Falling Short, U.S. Army Gets Creative with New Recruiting Strategy." *NPR Morning Edition,* 6 Jan. 2019, www.npr.org/2019/01/06/682608011/after-falling-short-u-s-army-gets-creative-with-new-recruiting-strategy.

Field, Kelly. "As Congress Prepares to Expand GI Bill, Colleges Reach Out to Veterans." *Chronicle of Higher Education,* 9 June 2008.

———. "Cost, Convenience Drive Veterans' College Choices." *Chronicle of Higher Education,* 25 Jul. 2008.

Fishman, Jenn, and Mary Jo Reiff. "Taking the High Road: Teaching for Transfer in an FYC Program." *Composition Forum*, vol. 18, 2008.

"508 compliance script for TPGS US 009: Accessing Higher Education." Joint Knowledge Online, jko.jten.mil/courses/tap/TGPS%20Standalone%20Training/CourseWare/TGPS-US009_Standalone/launch.html#.

Flores, Juan. "Latino Studies: New Contexts, New Concepts." *Harvard Educational Review,* vol. 67, no. 2, 1997, pp. 208–22.

Ford, Julie Dyke. "Integrating Communication into Engineering Curricula: An Interdisciplinary Approach to Facilitating Transfer at New Mexico Institute of Mining and Technology." *Composition Forum*, vol. 26, 2012.

Fulfilling the American Dream: Liberal Education and the Future of Work. American Association of Colleges and Universities, July 2018, www.aacu.org/sites/default/files/files/LEAP/2018EmployerResearchReport.pdf.

Gallagher, Matt. "How to Run a Successful Writing Workshop for Veterans." *New York Times,* 9 Sept. 2013, atwar.blogs.nytimes.com/2013/09/09/how-to-run-a-successful-writing-workshop-for-veterans.

———. *Kaboom: Embracing the Suck in a Savage Little War.* Da Capo Press, 2010.

———. *Youngblood: A Novel.* Washington Square Press, 2016.

Gates, Gary J. *Lesbian, Gay, and Bisexual Men and Women in the U.S. Military: Updated Estimates.* Williams Institute, UCLA School of Law, May 2010, escholarship.org/uc/item/0gn4t6t3. Accessed 10 Nov. 2019.

Gates, Gary J., and Jody L. Herman. "Transgender Military Service in the United States." *Williams Institute, UCLA School of Law*, May 2014, escholarship.org/uc/item/1t24j53h. Accessed 10 Nov. 2019.

"G.I. Bill of Rights." *National Archives Foundation*, www.archivesfounda tion.org/documents/g-i-bill-rights/.

Gibbs, Alan. *Contemporary American Trauma Narratives.* Edinburgh UP, 2014.

Giroux, Henry A. "The Militarization of U.S. Higher Education after 9/11." *Theory, Culture & Society,* vol. 25, no. 5, 2008, pp. 56–82.

Giroux, Henry A., and Kostas Myrsiades. *Beyond the Corporate University: Culture and Pedagogy in the New Millennium.* Rowman & Littlefield, 2001.

Glasser, Irene, John T. Powers, and William H. Zywiak. "Military Veterans at Universities: A Case of Culture Clash." *Anthropology News,* vol. 50, no. 5, May 2009, p. 33.

Goldbach, Jeremy T., and Carl Andrew Castro. "Lesbian, Gay, Bisexual, and Transgender (LGBT) Service Members: Life after Don't Ask, Don't Tell." *Current Psychiatry Reports,* vol. 18, no. 6, 2016.

Goldblatt, Eli. "Don't Call It Expressivism: Legacies of a 'Tacit Tradition.'" *College Composition and Communication,* vol. 68, no. 3, 2017, pp. 438–65.

Goldstein, Dana. "Should All Kids Go to College?" *The Nation,* 4–11 Jul. 2011.

Graf, Noreen M., Noel A. Ysasi, and Irmo Marini. "Assessment of Military Viewpoints Regarding Post-Secondary Education: Classroom Preferences and Experiences." *Rehabilitation Counseling Bulletin,* vol. 59, no.1, 2015, pp. 18–29.

Grasgreen, Allie. "Veterans Only." *Inside Higher Ed,* 4 Jan. 2012.

Gregg, Brian T., Dana M. Howell, and Anne Shordike. "Experiences of Veterans Transitioning to Postsecondary Education." *American Journal of Occupational Therapy,* vol. 70, no. 6, 2016, pp. 1–8.

Griffin, Kimberly A., and Claire K. Gilbert. "Better Transitions for Troops: An Application of Schlossberg's Transition Framework to Analyses of Barriers and Institutional Support Structures for Student Veterans." *The Journal of Higher Education,* vol. 86, no.1, Jan./Feb. 2015, pp. 71–97.

Grohowski, Mariana. "Moving Words/Words That Move: Language Practices Plaguing U.S. Servicewomen." *Women & Language,* vol. 37, no. 1, Spring 2014, pp. 121–30.

Grohowski, Mariana, and Alexis Hart. "Not Simply 'Freeing the Men to Fight': Rewriting the Reductive History of U.S. Military Women's

Achievements on and off the Battlefield." *Remembering Women Differently: Refiguring Rhetorical Work,* edited by Lynée Lewis Gaillet and Helen Gaillet Bailey. U of South Carolina P, 2019.

Hadlock, Erin D. *The Role of Genre, Identity, and Rhetorical Agency in the Military Writing of Post-9/11 Student-Veterans.* 2012. Colorado State U, MA thesis.

Hadlock, Erin, and Sue Doe. "Not Just 'Yes Sir, No Sir': How Genre and Agency Interact in Student-Veteran Writing." Doe and Langstraat, pp. 73–94.

Hagopian, Patrick. "Voices from Vietnam: Veterans' Oral Histories in the Classroom." *Journal of American History,* vol. 87, no. 2, Sept. 2000, pp. 593–601.

Hall, Kristin M. "Colleges Focus on Veterans as GI Bill Ups Numbers." *Community College Week,* vol. 21, no. 23, 27 Jul. 2009, pp. 8–9.

Hamrick, Florence A., and Corey B. Rumann. "Addressing the Needs of Women Servicemembers and Veterans in Higher Education." *On Campus with Women,* vol. 40, no. 3, 2012, pp. 1–5.

Handley, Derek G. "Stealth Veterans and Citizenship Pedagogy in the First Year Writing Classroom." *Reflections: A Journal of Public Rhetoric, Civic Writing, and Service Learning,* vol. 16, no. 2, 2016, pp. 106–27.

Harding, Scott, and Seth Kershner. *Counter-recruitment and the Campaign to Demilitarize Public Schools.* Palgrave Macmillan, 2015.

Harris, G. L. A., R. Finn Sumner, and Maria Carolina González-Prats. *Women Veterans: Lifting the Veil of Invisibility.* Routledge, 2018.

Hart, D. Alexis, and Roger Thompson. "'An Ethical Obligation': Promising Practices for Student Veterans in College Writing Classrooms." Conference on College Composition and Communication White Paper, June 2013. National Council of Teachers of English, prod-nctecdn.azureedge.net/nctefiles/groups/cccc/anethicalobligation.pdf.

———. "Veterans in the Writing Classroom: Three Programmatic Approaches to Facilitate the Transition from the Military to Higher Education." *College Composition and Communication,* vol. 68, no. 2, Dec. 2016, pp. 345–71.

———. "War, Trauma, and the Writing Classroom: A Response to Travis Martin's 'Combat in the Classroom.'" *Writing on the Edge,* vol. 23, no. 2, Spring 2013, pp. 37–47.

Hembrough, Tara. "Offering a First-Year Composition Classroom for Veterans and Cadets: A Learning-Community Model Case Study." *Journal of Veterans Studies,* vol. 2, no. 2, 2017, pp. 140–71.

Herbold, Hilary. "Never a Level Playing Field: Blacks and the G.I. Bill." *Journal of Blacks in Higher Education,* no. 6, Winter 1994–95, pp. 104–8.

Hicks, Louis, Eugenia L. Weiss, and Jose E. Coll. "Introduction to Veterans' Studies." *The Civilian Lives of U.S. Veterans: Issues and Identities,* edited by Hicks, Weiss, and Coll. ABC-CLIO, 2016, vol. 1, pp. 1–10.

Higgs, Robert. "Government and the Economy since World War II." Independent Institute Working Paper Number 58. Independent Institute, 20 Apr. 2005, www.independent.org/pdf/working_papers/58_government.pdf.

Hinton, Corrine. "'Front and Center': Marine Student-Veterans, Collaboration, and the Writing Center." Doe and Langstraat, pp. 257–81.

———. "'The Military Taught Me Something about Writing': How Student Veterans Complicate the Novice-to-Expert Continuum in First-Year Composition." *Composition Forum,* vol. 28, 2013.

"History and Timeline." US Department of Veterans Affairs, Veterans Benefits Administration, Education and Training, www.benefits.va.gov/gibill/history.asp.

Holm, Jeanne. *Women in the Military: An Unfinished Revolution.* Rev. ed. Presidio Press, 1992.

Horton, Alex. "On Getting By: Advice for College-Bound Vets." *Back to the Lake: A Reader for Writers,* edited by Thomas Cooley, 2nd ed., W. W. Norton, 2011.

"How Common Is PTSD in Veterans?" US Department of Veterans Affairs, Center for PTSD, www.ptsd.va.gov/understand/common/common_veterans.asp.

Hughes, Trevor. "Vets Go from Combat to Campus." *USA Today,* 12 Apr. 2011.

Humes, Edward. "How the GI Bill Shunted Blacks into Vocational Training." *Journal of Blacks in Higher Education,* no. 53, Autumn 2006, 92–104.

Hunt, Nigel, and Ian Robbins. "Telling Stories of the War: Ageing Veterans Coping with Their Memories through Narrative." *Oral History,* vol. 26, no. 2, Autumn 1998, pp. 57–64.

"'I Am a Post-9/11 *Student* Veteran': Collaboration of the Institute of Veterans and Military Families and Student Veterans of America." Higher Education Institute, 2017, ivmf.syracuse.edu/wp.../I-Am-a-Post-911-Student-Veteran-Report.pdf.

Investing in Futures: Public Higher Education in America. City U of New York, www.laguardiawagnerarchive.lagcc.cuny.edu/FileBrowser.aspx?LinkToFile=FILES_DOC/CALENDARS/2010_Investing_In_Futures.pdf.

Jenner, Brandy M. "Student Veterans and the Transition to Higher Education: Integrating Existing Literatures." *Journal of Veterans Studies,* vol. 2, no. 2, 2017, pp. 26–44.

Jones, Kevin C. "Understanding Student Veterans in Transition." *The Qualitative Report,* vol. 18, no. 37, 2013, pp. 1–14.

———. "Understanding Transition Experiences of Combat Veterans Attending Community College." *Community College Journal of Research and Practice,* vol. 41, no. 2, 2017, pp. 107–23.

Jones, Kevin C., and Bonnie K. Fox Garrity. "For-Profit Institutions and Student Veteran Data." *New Directions for Institutional Research,* vol. 2016, no. 171, 2017, pp. 75–85.

Kalama, Jaycee. "OSU Helps Veterans Transition to College." *Daily Barometer* [Oregon State U], 13 Nov. 2018, www.orangemedianet work.com/daily_barometer/osu-helps-veterans-transition-to-college/article_4b3d31b2-e6c7-11e8-97f6-33fc24cad39e.html.

Kamara, Hassan. "Writing: A Way to Maximize Returns on the Army's Investments in Education." *Military Review,* Jan.–Feb. 2017, pp. 114–21.

Karaali, Gizem. "An Ode to Teacherless Writing Classes." *Inside Higher Ed,* 2 Jan. 2019.

Kato, Lorrie, et al. "From Combat Zones to the Classroom: Transitional Adjustment in OEF/OIF Student Veterans." *The Qualitative Report,* vol. 21, no. 11, 2016, pp. 2131–47.

Keast, Darren. "A Class for Vets, Not by a Vet: Developing a Veteran-Friendly Composition Course at City College of San Francisco." *Composition Forum,* vol. 28, 2013.

Keller, Jared. "The U.S. Military Has Always Been a Social Experiment." *Task & Purpose,* 13 Dec. 2017, taskandpurpose.com/us-military-social-experiment.

Kennedy, Kristen. "Perspectives: The Fourth Generation." *College Composition and Communication,* vol. 59, no. 3, 2008, pp. 525–37.

Kidder, Tracy. "Soldiers of Misfortune: A Report on the Veterans of Vietnam—and on the Often Disgraceful Treatment They Have Received from Their Countrymen." *The Atlantic,* March 1978.

Kiely, Denis O., and Lisa Swift. "Casualties of War: Combat Trauma and the Return of the Combat Veteran." *Teaching English in the Two-Year College,* vol. 36, no. 4, May 2009, pp. 357–64.

Kim, Young M., and James S. Cole. *Student Veterans/Service Members' Engagement in College and University Life and Education.* American Council on Education and National Survey of Student Engagement, 2013.

Klay, Phil. "After War, a Failure of the Imagination." *New York Times,* 8 Feb. 2014.

Klein, Robert E. *Women Veterans: Past, Present and Future.* Rev. ed. US Department of Veterans Affairs, 2005.

Kopelson, Karen. "Sp(l)itting Images; or, Back to the Future of (Rhetoric and?) Composition." *College Composition and Communication,* vol. 59, no. 4, June 2008, pp. 750–80.

LaFrance, Adrienne. "Millennials Are Out-Reading Older Generations." *The Atlantic,* 10 Sept. 2014.

Lanzmann, Claude. "The Obscenity of Understanding: An Evening with Claude Lanzmann." *Trauma: Explorations in Memory,* edited by Cathy Caruth. Johns Hopkins UP, 1995, pp. 200–19.

"A Leader's Guide to After-Action Reviews." US Department of the Army, Headquarters, Sept. 1993, www.acq.osd.mil/dpap/ccap/cc/jcchb/Files/Topical/After_Action_Report/resources/tc25-20.pdf.

Leonhardy, Galen. "Transformations: Working with Veterans in the Composition Classroom." *Teaching English in the Two-Year College,* vol. 36, no. 4, 2009, pp. 339–52.

Levinson, Leila. *Gated Grief: The Daughter of a G.I. Concentration Camp Liberator Discovers a Legacy of Trauma.* Cable Books, 2011.

Lieberman, Drew, and Kathryn Stewart. *Strengthening Perceptions of America's Post-9/11 Veterans: Survey Analysis Report.* Greenberg Quinlan Rosner Research, 17 June 2014, https://www.dillonconsult.com/wp-content/uploads/2013/03/Strengthening-Perceptions-of-Americas-Post-911-Veterans-Survey-Analysis-Report-Got-Your-6-June-2014.pdf.

Lim, Jae Hoon, et al. "Invisible Cultural Barriers: Contrasting Perspectives on Student Veterans' Transition." *Journal of College Student Development,* vol. 59, no. 3, 2018, pp. 291–308.

Linehan, Adam. "The Recruiters: Searching for The Next Generation of Warfighters in a Divided America." *Task & Purpose,* 28 Nov. 2017, taskandpurpose.com/east-orange-army-recruitment-divided-america.

Livingston, Wade G., et al. "Coming Home: Student Veterans' Articulation of College Re-enrollment." *Journal of Student Affairs Research and Practice,* vol. 48, no. 3, 2011, pp. 315–31.

Lucas, Janet. "Getting Personal: Responding to Student Self-Disclosure." *Teaching English in the Two-Year College,* vol. 34, no. 4, May 2007, pp. 367–79.

Malenczyk, Rita, et al., editors. *Composition, Rhetoric, and Disciplinarity.* Utah State UP, 2018.

Mallory, Angie, and Doug Downs. "Uniform Meets Rhetoric: Excellence through Interaction." Doe and Langstraat, pp. 51–72.

Marcus, Jon. "Community Colleges Rarely Graduate the Veterans They Recruit." *The Atlantic,* 21 Apr. 2017.

Martin, Travis L. "Combat in the Classroom." *Writing on the Edge*, vol. 22, no. 2, 2012, pp. 27–35.

McBain, Lesley, et al. *From Soldier to Student II: Assessing Campus Programs for Veterans and Service Members*. American Council on Education, 2012.

McCormick, Patrick T. "Volunteers and Incentives: Buying the Bodies of the Poor." *Journal of the Society of Christian Ethics*, vol. 27, no. 1, 2007, pp. 77–93.

McGregor, Bree, and Lourdes Fernandez. "Writing Faculty on the Marine Corps Base: Building Strong Classroom Communities through Engagement and Advocacy." *Reflections*, vol. 16, no. 2, Fall 2016, pp. 129–50.

McGregor, Jena. "Military Women in Combat: Why Making It Official Matters." Barnet and Bedau, pp. 28–31.

McLagan, Meg, and Daria Sommers, producers and directors. *Lioness*. Docurama Films, 2008.

McMurray, Andrew J. "College Students, the G.I. Bill, and the Proliferation of Online Learning: A History of Learning and Contemporary Challenges." *The Internet and Higher Education*, vol. 10, no. 2, 2007, pp. 143–50.

Meehan, Shannon. "Why We Don't Need a Parade: One Vet's Dissent." *New York Daily News*, 5 Mar. 2012.

Meehan, Shannon P., with Roger Thompson. *Beyond Duty: Life on the Frontline in Iraq*. Polity Press, 2009.

Micciche, Laura R. "More Than a Feeling: Disappointment and WPA Work." *College English*, vol. 64, no. 4, 2002, pp. 432–58.

"Military Benefits." College Board, CLEP, clep.collegeboard.org/earn-college-credit/military-benefits.

The Military-Civilian Gap: War and Sacrifice in the Post-9/11 Era. Pew Social & Demographic Trends, 2011.

The Military Guide: About the Guide to the Evaluation of Educational Experiences in the Armed Services. American Council on Education, www.acenet.edu/Programs-Services/Pages/Credit-Transcripts/military-guide-online.aspx.

Molina, Dani. "Higher Ed Spotlight: Undergraduate Student Veterans." American Council on Education, 2014, www.acenet.edu/news-room/Pages/Higher-Ed-Spotlight-Undergraduate-Student-Veterans.aspx.

Monahan, Evelyn, and Rosemary Neidel-Greenlee. *A Few Good Women: America's Military Women from World War I to the Wars in Iraq and Afghanistan*. Knopf, 2010.

Money, Karina. *Transitioning from Military to College: A Pilot Course Developed for Veterans to Help Them Succeed in Their First Year of College.* 2015. Northeastern U, PhD dissertation.

Moore, Ellen. *Grateful Nation: Student Veterans and the Rise of the Military-Friendly Campus.* Duke UP, 2017.

Morgan, Dan. "Ethical Issues Raised by Students' Personal Writing." *College English,* vol. 60, no. 3, March 1998, pp. 318–25.

Morreale, Cathleen. *Academic Motivation and Academic Self-Concept: Military Veteran Students in Higher Education.* 2011. State U of New York at Buffalo, PhD dissertation.

Motta, Robert W., et al. "Secondary Trauma: Assessing Inter-generational Transmission of War Experiences with a Modified Stroop Procedure." *Journal of Clinical Psychology,* vol. 53, no. 8, Dec. 1997, pp. 895–903.

Mueller, Derek. "Grasping Rhetoric and Composition by Its Long Tail: What Graphs Can Tell Us about the Field's Changing Shape." *College Composition and Communication,* vol. 64, no. 1, Sept. 2012, pp. 195–223.

Mulhall, Erin. *Women Warriors: Supporting She 'Who Has Borne the Battle.'* Iraq and Afghanistan Veterans of America, 2009.

Naphan, Dara, and Marta Elliot. "Role Exit from the Military: Student Veterans' Perceptions of Transitioning from the U.S. Military to Higher Education." *The Qualitative Report,* vol. 20, no. 2, 2015, pp. 36–48.

National Center for Veterans Analysis and Statistics. *Profile of Veterans: 2016.* US Department of Veterans Affairs, www.va.gov/vetdata/docs/SpecialReports/Profile_of_Veterans_2016.pdf.

———. *Profile of Women Veterans: 2016.* US Department of Veterans Affairs, www.va.gov/vetdata/docs/SpecialReports/Women_Veterans_Profile_12_22_2016.pdf.

National Defense Research Institute. *Sexual Orientation and U.S. Military Personnel Policy: An Update of RAND's 1993 Study.* RAND, 2010.

National Economic Council and the President's Council of Economic Advisers. *The Fast Track: Streamlining Credentialing and Licensing for Service Members, Veterans, and Their Spouses.* Executive Office of the President, 2013, www.credentialingexcellence.org/d/do/771.

"National Survey of Veterans, Active Duty Service Members, Demobilized National Guard and Reserve Members, Family Members, and Surviving Spouses." US Department of Veterans Affairs, 18 Oct. 2010, www.va.gov/vetdata/docs/surveysandstudies/nvssurveyfinalweightedreport.pdf.

Navarre Cleary, Michelle. "What WPAs Need to Know to Prepare New Teachers to Work with Adult Students." *WPA Journal,* vol. 32, no. 1, Fall 2008, pp. 113–28.

Navarre Cleary, Michelle, and Kathryn Wozniak. "Veterans as Adult Learners in Composition Courses." *Composition Forum,* vol. 28, 2013.

"NEH Launches New *Standing Together* Initiative." National Endowment for the Humanities, 2 Apr. 2014, www.neh.gov/news/press-release/2014-04-02.

Nelson, Cary. "What Hath English Wrought: The Corporate University's Fast Food Discipline." *Disciplining English: Alternative Histories, Critical Perspectives,* edited by David R. Shumway and Craig Dionne. SUNY P, 2002, pp. 195–211.

Nelson, Luke R. "Combating For-Profit Education's Use of Erroneous, Deceptive, and Misleading Practices against Veterans and the GI Bill." *Mitchell Hamline Law Review,* vol. 43, 2017, pp. 505–40.

"Nontraditional Undergraduates: Definitions and Data." National Center for Education Statistics, nces.ed.gov/pubs/web/97578e.asp.

Nowacek, Rebecca S. *Agents of Integration: Understanding Transfer as a Rhetorical Act.* Southern Illinois UP, 2011.

Olsen, Timothy, Karen Badger, and Michael D. McCuddy. "Understanding the Student Veterans' College Experience: An Exploratory Study." *U.S. Army Medical Department Journal,* Oct.-Dec. 2014, pp. 101–08.

"One Million Now Benefit from Post-9/11 GI Bill." *Veterans Today Archives,* 8 Nov. 2013, https://www.veteranstodayarchives.com/2013/11/08/one-million-now-benefit-from-post-911-gi-bill/.

Onkst, David H. "'First a Negro . . . Incidentally a Veteran': Black World War Two Veterans and the G.I. Bill of Rights in the Deep South, 1944–1948." *Journal of Social History,* vol. 31, no. 3, 1998, pp. 517–43.

Osborne, Nicholas J. "Veteran Ally: Practical Strategies for Closing the Military-Civilian Gap on Campus." *Innovative Higher Education,* vol. 39, no. 3, 2014, pp. 247–60.

Ottley, Alford H. "Empty Promise: Black American Veterans and the New G.I. Bill." *New Directions for Adult and Continuing Education,* vol. 2014, no. 144, 2014, pp. 79–88.

Paris, Django, and H. Samy Alim. "What Are We Seeking to Sustain through Culturally Sustaining Pedagogy? A Loving Critique Forward." *Harvard Educational Review,* vol. 84, no. 1, Spring 2014, pp. 85–100.

Patton, Jaclyn. "Encouraging Exploitation of the Military by For-Profit Colleges: The New G.I. Bill and the 90/10 Rule." *South Texas Law Review,* vol. 54, 2012, pp. 425–49.

Pennebaker, James W. "Writing about Emotional Experiences as a Therapeutic Process." *Psychological Science,* vol. 8, no. 3, May 1997, pp. 162–66.

Perkins, D. N., and Gavriel Salomon. "Are Cognitive Skills Context-Bound?" *Educational Researcher,* vol. 18, no. 1, 1989, pp. 16–25.

———. "The Science and Art of Transfer." *If Minds Matter: A Foreword to the Future,* edited by Arthur L. Costa, James A. Bellanca, and Robin Fogarty, vol. 1, *Rationale for Change,* Skylight Professional Development, 1991, pp. 201–10.

Phelps, Louise Wetherbee, and John M. Ackerman. "Making the Case for Disciplinarity in Rhetoric, Composition, and Writing Studies: The Visibility Project." *College Composition and Communication,* vol. 62, no. 1, 2010, pp. 180–215.

Phillips, Glenn A., and Yvonna S. Lincoln. "Introducing Veteran Critical Theory." *International Journal of Qualitative Studies in Education,* vol. 30, no. 7, 2017, pp. 656–68.

"Post-9/11 G.I. Bill Yellow Ribbon FAQs." Department of Veterans Affairs, 2012, benefits.va.gov/gibill/docs/factsheets/2012_Yellow_Rib bon_Student_FAQs.pdf.

Queen, Barbara, Laurie Lewis, and John Ralph. *Services and Support Programs for Military Service Members at Postsecondary Institutions, 2012–13: First Look.* National Center for Education Statistics, 2014, nces.ed.gov /pubs2014/2014017.pdf.

Raab, F. Dean. *For-Profit Colleges and the GI Bill: A Worthwhile Investment?* US Department of Justice, 2012.

Radford, Alexandria Walton. *Military Service Members and Veterans: A Profile of Those Enrolled in Undergraduate and Graduate Education in 2007–08.* National Center for Education Statistics, Sept. 2011, nces .ed.gov/pubs2011/2011163.pdf.

"Resolution 3: Encouraging Communication about the War." Conference on College Composition and Communication (CCCC) Executive Committee, 22 Mar. 2003. National Council of Teachers of English, www.ncte.org/cccc/resolutions/2003.

Roff, Sarah. "Treatment, Not Trigger Warnings." *Chronicle of Higher Education,* 23 May 2014.

Rojas, Fabio. *From Black Power to Black Studies: How a Radical Social Movement Became an Academic Discipline.* Johns Hopkins UP, 2007.

"The Role of the School Certifying Official." *Military Advanced Education and Transition,* vol. 8, no. 6, 22 Jul. 2013, pp. 11–13.

Romey, Andy. "SVA Nearing Release of G.I. Bill Graduation Rates."

American Legion Online Newsletter, 8 Jan. 2014, www.legion.org/edu cation/218173/sva-nearing-release-gi-bill-graduation-rates.

Rose, Sarah F. "The Right to a College Education? The G.I. Bill, Public Law 16, and Disabled Veterans." *Journal of Policy History,* vol. 24, no. 1, 2012, pp. 26–52.

Rothberg, Michael. "A Failure of the Imagination: Diagnosing the Post-9/11 Novel: A Response to Richard Gray." *American Literary History,* vol. 21, no. 1, 2009, pp. 152–58.

Rumann, Corey B., and Florence A. Hamrick. "Student Veterans in Transition: Re-enrolling after War Zone Deployments." *Journal of Higher Education,* vol. 81, no. 4, 2010, pp. 431–58.

Ryan, Shawn W., et al. "From Boots to Books: Applying Schlossberg's Model to Transitioning American Veterans." *NACADA Journal,* vol. 31, no. 1, 2011, pp. 55–63.

Salemme, Christopher J. "Unpatriotic Profit: How For-Profit Colleges Target Veterans and What the Government Must Do to Stop Them." *Brigham Young University Journal of Public Law,* vol. 32, no. 1, 2017, pp. 89–116.

Saltmarsh, John. "Changing Pedagogies." *Handbook of Engaged Scholarship: Contemporary Landscapes, Future Directions,* vol. 1, *Institutional Change,* edited by Hiram E. Fitzgerald, Cathy Burack, and Sarena D. Seifer, Michigan State UP, 2010, pp. 331–52.

Sander, Libby. "Veterans Tell Elite Colleges: 'We Belong.'" *Chronicle of Higher Education,* 7 Jan. 2013.

Santovec, Mary Lou. "Women Veterans: 'Invisible Warriors' on Your Campus." *Women in Higher Education,* vol. 21, no, 11, 2012, pp. 29–30.

———. "Women Vets: An Underserved Population." *Women in Higher Education,* vol. 24, no. 1, 2015, pp. 1–2.

Scharf, Miri. "Long-Term Effects of Trauma: Psychosocial Functioning of the Second and Third Generation of Holocaust Survivors." *Development and Psychopathology,* vol. 19, no. 2, Apr. 2007, pp. 603–22.

Schell, Eileen E. "Writing the Way Home: Creative Nonfiction and Digital Circulation in a Veterans' Writing Group." *Getting Personal: Teaching Personal Writing in the Digital Age,* edited by Laura Gray-Rosendale. SUNY P, 2018, pp. 21–42.

———. "Writing with Veterans in a Community Writing Group." *Composition Forum,* vol. 28, 2013.

Schell, Eileen E., and Ivy Kleinbart. "'I Have to Speak Out': Writing with Veterans in a Community Writing Group." Doe and Langstraat, pp. 119–39.

Schlossberg, Nancy K. "A Model for Analyzing Human Adaptation to Transition." *Counseling Psychologist,* vol. 9, no. 2, 1981, pp. 2–18.

Schlossberg, Nancy K., Ann Q. Lynch, and Arthur W. Chickering. *Improving Higher Education Environments for Adults: Responsive Programs and Services from Entry to Departure.* Jossey-Bass, 1989.

Schwehm, Jeremy S. "Do Student Demographics and Community College Experiences Influence the Adjustment Process of Adult Vertical Transfer Students?" *Community College Enterprise,* vol. 23, no. 1, 2017, pp. 9–25.

Sewall, Michael. "Veterans Use New G.I. Bill Largely at For-Profit and Two-Year Colleges." *Chronicle of Higher Education,* 13 June 2010, pp. A20-A21.

Shackelford, Allan L. "Documenting the Needs of Student Veterans with Disabilities: Intersection Roadblocks, Solutions, and Legal Realities." *Journal of Postsecondary Education and Disability,* vol. 22, no. 1, 2009, pp. 36–42.

Shane, Leo. "VA Secretary Calls Texas Shooter a Criminal, Not a Veteran." *Military Times,* 6 Nov. 2017, www.militarytimes.com/veterans/2017/11/06/va-secretary-calls-texas-shooter-a-criminal-not-a-veteran/.

Skinnell, Ryan. "Enlisting Composition: How First-Year Composition Helped Reorient Higher Education in the G.I. Bill Era." *Journal of Veterans Studies,* vol. 2, no. 1, 2017, pp. 79–84.

Sloane, Wick. "Annual Veterans Count, 2013." *Inside Higher Ed,* 11 Nov. 2013.

———. "Veterans Day 2012." *Inside Higher Ed,* 12 Nov. 2012.

Sogunro, Olusegun Agboola. "Motivating Factors for Adult Learners in Higher Education." *International Journal of Higher Education,* vol. 4, no. 1, 2015, pp. 22–37.

Solaro, Erin. *Women in the Line of Fire: What You Should Know about Women in the Military.* Seal Press, 2006.

S[ommers], J[eff]. "Editorial: Teaching War Stories." *Teaching English in the Two-Year College,* vol. 36, no. 4, 2009, pp. 337–38.

Steele, Jennifer L., Nicholas Salcedo, and James Coley. *Service Members in School: Military Veterans' Experiences Using the Post-9/11 G.I. Bill and Pursuing Postsecondary Education.* RAND/ACE, 2010.

Stone, Sharon L. M. "Internal Voices, External Constraints: Exploring the Impact of Military Service on Student Development." *Journal of College Student Development,* vol. 58, no. 3, 2017, pp. 365–84.

Street, Mark. "Military Veterans Bring Value to the Classroom." *Chronicle of Higher Education,* 21 Apr. 2014.

Stripling, Jack. "Tillman's Legacy." *Inside Higher Ed,* 12 Mar. 2010.

"Student Veterans: A Valuable Asset to Higher Education." Syracuse U Institute for Veteran and Military Families and Student Veterans of America, June 2017, ivmf.syracuse.edu/wp-content/uploads/2017/09/Student-Veterans_Valuable_9.8.17_NEW.pdf.

"Student Veterans in the College Composition Classroom: Realizing Their Strengths and Assessing Their Needs." Conference on College Composition and Communication, Mar. 2015, cccc.ncte.org/cccc/resources/positions/student-veterans.

Sura, Thomas. "Articulating Veteran-Friendly: Preparing First-Year Writing Instructors to Work with Veterans." *Reflections,* vol. 16, no. 2, 2016, pp. 187–206.

Swearingen, C. Jan. "Rhetoric and Composition as a Coherent Intellectual Discipline: A Meditation." *Rhetoric and Composition as Intellectual Work,* edited by Gary A. Olson, Southern Illinois UP, 2002, pp. 12–22.

Szymendera, Scott D. "'Who Is a 'Veteran?': Basic Eligibility for Veterans' Benefits." Congressional Research Service Report for Congress, 25 May 2016, fas.org/sgp/crs/misc/R42324.pdf.

Tanielian, Terri, et al. "Invisible Wounds: Mental Health and Cognitive Care Needs of America's Returning Veterans." RAND, 2008, www.rand.org/pubs/research_briefs/RB9336.html.

Taylor, Alexander, Rodney Parks, and Ashley Edwards. "Challenges on the Front Lines: Serving Today's Student Veterans." *College and University,* vol. 91, no. 4, 2016, pp. 47–60.

The Tongue and Quill: Communication Is an Essential Tool for the Twenty-First Century Air Force. Air Force Handbook 33–337, 30 June 1997, US Department of the Air Force, apps.dtic.mil/dtic/tr/fulltext/u2/a404949.pdf. Rev. May 27, 2015. static.e-publishing.af.mil/production/1/saf_cio_a6/publication/afh33-337/afh33-337.pdf.

Thompson, Roger. "The Tyranny of Best Practices: Structural Violence and Writing Programs." *JAEPL,* vol. 23, Winter 2017–18, pp. 38–55.

"Training Tracks." US Department of Defense, Transition Assistance Program, webdm.dmdc.osd.mil/dodtap/tracks.html.

"Transfer Post-9/11 G.I. Bill to Spouse and Dependents." US Department of Veterans Affairs, www.benefits.va.gov/gibill/post911_transfer.asp.

"Transition Assistance Program (TAP) Information." US Department of Labor, www.dol.gov/agencies/vets/programs/tap.

Trzinski, Zach. "Not All Veterans Are the Same." *See Me for Who I Am: Student Veterans' Stories of War and Coming Home,* edited by David Chrisinger, Hudson Whitman/Excelsior College P, 2016, pp. 114–20.

Turner, Sarah, and John Bound. "Closing the Gap or Widening the Divide: The Effects of the G.I. Bill and World War II on the Educational Outcomes of Black Americans." *Journal of Economic History,* vol. 63, no. 1, 2003, pp. 145–77.

"2015 Demographics: Profile of the Military Community." *Military One Source,* download.militaryonesource.mil/12038/MOS/Reports/2015-Demographics-Report.pdf.

2015 Veteran Economic Opportunity Report. US Department of Veterans Affairs, www.benefits.va.gov/benefits/docs/veteraneconomicopportunity report2015.pdf.

United States. Congress. Senate Committee on Health, Labor, and Pensions. *For Profit Higher Education: The Failure to Safeguard the Federal Investment and Ensure Student Success.* US GPO, 2012.

Vaccaro, Annemarie. "'It's Not One Size Fits All': Diversity *among* Student Veterans." *Journal of Student Affairs Research and Practice,* vol. 52, no. 4, 2015, pp. 347–58.

Vacchi, David T. "Considering Student Veterans on the Twenty-First-Century College Campus." *About Campus,* vol. 17, no. 2, 2012, pp. 15–21.

Vacchi, David T., and Joseph B. Berger. "Student Veterans in Higher Education." *Higher Education: Handbook of Theory and Research,* vol. 29, edited by Michael B. Paulsen. Springer, 2014, pp. 93–151.

Valentino, Marilyn J. "CCCC Chair's Address: Rethinking the Fourth *C:* Call to Action." *College Composition and Communication,* vol. 62, no. 2, Dec. 2010, pp. 364–78.

———. "Responding When a Life Depends on It: What to Write in the Margins When Students Self-Disclose." Conference on College Composition and Communication, 24 Mar. 1995, Washington, DC.

———. "Serving Those Who Have Served: Preparing for Student Veterans in Our Writing Programs, Classes and Writing Centers." *WPA Journal,* vol. 36, no. 1, Fall/Winter 2012, pp. 164–78.

"Veteran's Essay on Killing." *Baltimore Sun,* 21 Nov. 2010.

"Veterans' Success Jam: Ensuring Success for Returning Veterans." American Council on Education, www.acenet.edu/news-room/Pages/Veterans-Jam-2010.aspx.

Walker, Childs. "War Veteran Barred from CCBC Campus for Frank Words on Killing." *Baltimore Sun,* 20 Nov. 2010.

Wardle, Elizabeth. "Understanding Transfer from FYC: Preliminary Results of a Longitudinal Study." *WPA Journal,* vol. 31, no. 1–2, Fall/Winter 2007, pp. 65–85.

Weaver, Richard M. *The Ethics of Rhetoric.* 1953. Routledge, 2009.

Weiss, Eugenia L. "Building Community in a Diverse College Class-room." Coll and Weiss, pp. 104–29.

Weisser, Christian, Michelle Ballif, Alexis Hart, and Roger Thompson. "From the Editors." *Composition Forum*, vol. 28, 2013.

"What Is Moral Injury." Syracuse U Moral Injury Project, moralinjury project.syr.edu/about-moral-injury/.

Wheeler, Holly A. "Veterans' Transitions to Community College: A Case Study." *Community College Journal of Research and Practice*, vol. 36, no. 10, 2012, pp. 775–92.

Williams Mlynarczyk, Rebecca. "Personal and Academic Writing: Revisiting the Debate." *Journal of Basic Writing*, vol. 25, no. 1, 2006, pp. 4–25.

Wilson, Kristin Bailey. "Thank You for Your Service: Military Initiatives on College Campuses." *New Horizons in Adult Education and Human Resource Development*, vol. 26, no. 3, 2014, pp. 54–60.

Wilson, Kristin B., et al. "When the Army Post Is the Campus: Understanding the Social and Academic Integration of Soldiers Attending College." *Journal of College Student Development*, vol. 54, no. 6, 2013, pp. 628–42.

Wilson, Nancy Effinger, and Micah Wright. "Writing Center Tutor Corps: A Veterans-Tutoring-Veterans Program." *WLN: A Journal of Writing Center Scholarship*, vol. 41, no. 9–10, 2017, pp. 2–10.

Wilson, Robert M., et al. "Military Veterans Sharing First-Person Stories of War and Homecoming: A Pathway to Social Engagement, Personal Healing, and Public Understanding of Veterans' Issues." *Smith College Studies in Social Work*, vol. 79, no. 3–4, July–Dec. 2009, pp. 392–432.

Woll, Pamela. *Teaching America's Best: Preparing Your Classrooms to Welcome Returning Veterans and Service Members.* Give an Hour and National Organization on Disability, 2010.

"Women and the Draft." US Selective Service System, ww.sss.gov/Registration/Women-And-Draft.

Wong, Alia. "'Dollar Signs in Uniform': Why For-Profit Colleges Target Veterans." *The Atlantic*, 24 June 2015.

Wright, Micah. *Improvise, Adapt, and Overcome: The Student Veteran and Considerations of Identity, Space, and Pedagogy.* 2013. Texas State U, MA thesis.

Yancey, Kathleen Blake. *Writing in the 21st Century.* National Council of Teachers of English, 2009.

Yancey, Kathleen Blake, Liane Robertson, and Kara Taczak. *Writing across Contexts: Transfer, Composition, and Sites of Writing.* Utah State UP, 2014.

Zinger, Lana, and Andrea Cohen. "Veterans Returning from War into the Classroom: How Can Colleges Be Better Prepared to Meet Their Needs." *Contemporary Issues in Education Research,* vol. 3, no. 1, 2010, pp. 39–52.

Zipin, Lew. "Dark Funds of Knowledge, Deep Funds of Pedagogy: Exploring Boundaries between Lifeworlds and Schools." *Discourse: Studies in the Cultural Politics of Education,* vol. 30, no. 3, 2009, pp. 317–31.

INDEX

transitioning. *See* transition(s)
tropes dominating portraits of, xxii
Veterans Administration (VA), xix
"Veterans Day Speech" (Shi), 37–39
veterans' lounges, 123–24
veterans resource officer (VRO),
122–24
veterans studies (VS). *See also* writing
(veterans) studies
advocacy groups, 2
asset-based approach to, xxv–xxvii,
93, 129–32
challenges of, 3–4
deficit training models, xxv, 129
defining, xx
degree programs, 1
emergence of, 1
scholarship, 1–2
variables, xvii–xviii
veterans studies (VS) within writing
studies (WS). *See* writing
(veterans) studies
veteran students. *See* student veteran
veterans-tutoring-veterans programs,
124
Veterans Writing Project, xxvii
Vietnam veterans, 73, 96, 140n4
vocational training model, 25–27

Wardle, Elizabeth, 31
"War: No Place to Hide" (Oetting),
40–46
war trauma. *See also* combat veteran
depathologizing, 105–6
engaging in the classroom, 93–98
healing through writing about,
96–97
perpetrator, 94–96
sexual violence as, 95
storytelling strategy for resolving,
96–97
war trauma, disclosing
acknowledging, 102–3
assessment and, 103

challenges for instructors, 94
ethical responses, 96–98
hazards and benefits, 98–99
methods for responding to,
98–105
principles for responding to,
100–105
reporting, 104–5
trust required for, 103–4
Weiss, Eugenia, 129, 145n4
Wheeler, Holly, 71, 139n22–23
Whittington, Charles, 98
Wilson, Kristin, 70, 72, 125
Wilson, Nancy Effinger, 124
Woll, Pamela, 129
women veterans
active duty statistics, 20
demographics, 8
GI Bill benefits, eligibility for, 20
isolation, feelings of, 9
male veterans, willingness to work
with, 9
military service, historically, 20–21
self-identification as, xxi, 9
stereotype vs. reality of, 8–9
writing workshops for, xxvii
Words after War, xxvii
work ethic, 35
Wozniak, Kathryn, 76
Wright, Micah, 124
writing (veterans) studies
emergence of, xxvii, xxviii, 6
ethical obligations, 4, 96–98,
141n10
formation of, 2–3
scholarship, 4–5
teacher-scholars, 4–6
writing (veterans) studies, guiding
principles
demographics affect campus
culture and writing classrooms,
7–11
not all institutions or writing
programs need a systemic

AUTHORS

D. Alexis Hart is an associate professor of English, director of writing, and director of First Year Experience at Allegheny College, where she teaches an introduction to literature course focused on post-9/11 war literature and a community-engaged seminar that connects first-year college students with local military members and veteran-focused organizations. A US Navy veteran, Hart commissioned through Naval ROTC at the University of Rochester as a Supply Corps officer in 1993. After receiving her professional training at the Navy Supply Corps School (NSCS) in Athens, Georgia, Hart reported to her first ship, the USS *Essex* (LHD-2) in San Diego in 1994. After 36 months aboard the *Essex*, she returned to Athens as an instructor at NSCS. While serving at NSCS, Hart began attending graduate school at the University of Georgia (UGA). In 1999, she resigned her commission and began attending UGA full-time and earned her PhD in rhetoric and composition in 2003. Hart is a co-founder of the CCCC Writing with Former, Current, and Future Members of the Military Standing Group, served as co-chair of the CCCC Task Force on Veterans, and was competitively selected to participate in the 2016 National Endowment for the Humanities Summer Institute themed "Veterans in Society: Ambiguities and Representations" held at Virginia Tech. At Allegheny, Hart is the faculty advisor for the Army ROTC club and the Allegheny Veterans Services student group.

Roger Thompson is associate professor and director of the Program in Writing and Rhetoric at Stony Brook University. His previous books include *Emerson and the History of Rhetoric* and *No Word for Wilderness*. He is Senior Fellow with Syracuse University's Institute for Veterans and Military Families, and he consults with colleges and universities on veteran issues. He has lectured by invitation at schools across the country on war, veteran transitions, and trauma, and he has conducted trainings for the US Army in Germany and the National Traumatic Brain Injury Center in Johnstown, Pennsylvania. Thompson is currently pursuing work on Iraq War memoirs.

BOOKS IN THE CCCC STUDIES IN WRITING & RHETORIC SERIES

This book was typeset in Garamond and Frutiger by Barbara Frazier.
Typefaces used on the cover include Garamond and News Gothic.
The book was printed on 50-lb. White Offset paper
by Seaway Printing Company, Inc.